Home Filing
Made Easy!

Mary E. Martin, CFP
J.Michael Martin, JD, CFP

Dearborn
Financial Publishing, Inc.

While a great deal of care has been taken to provide accurate and current information, the ideas, suggestions, general principles and conclusions presented in this text are subject to local, state and federal laws and regulations, court cases and any revisions of same. The reader is thus urged to consult legal counsel regarding any points of law—this publication should not be used as a substitute for competent legal advice.

Dearborn Financial Publishing, Inc.
Publisher: Kathleen A. Welton
Associate Editor: Karen A. Christensen
Interior and Cover Design: Sean M. Martin

Published by Dearborn Financial Publishing, Inc. and
          Financial Advantage, Inc.

Printed in the United States of America

94 95 96 10 9 8 7 6 5 4 3 2 1

Library of Congress Cataloging-in-Publication Data

Martin, Mary E., 1941–
    Home filing made easy! / Mary E. Martin and J. Michael Martin
        p.   cm. — (The Financial Advantage series)
    Includes index.
    ISBN 0-79310-610-9
    1. Finance, Personal. 2. Filing systems. 3. Records—Management.
    I. Martin, J. Michael 1941– . II. Title. III. Series.
    HG179.M3435 1993
    640—dc20   93-23763
                                                            CIP

For information about quantity pricing or custom versions:

P.O. Box 1870
Ellicott City, Maryland 21041-1870
800-466-3453

To the world's "savers" for whom caution is the only sensible way of life!

Mary

Mary (a certified saver)

To the stalwart "thrower-outers" for whom efficiency is critical to good life!

Mike

Mike (an unabashed thrower-outer)

May you find here the golden mean!

What the Media Says...

"HOMEFILE® is truly ingenious; this is the best system you can buy for arranging important personal papers."
New Choices for Retirement Living

"...give yourself the gift of organization with HOMEFILE®, an easy-to-use filing system...the quickest way we've found to put an end to your financial paper flood."
Elizabeth Birkelund Oberbeck
"Money Talk," **Cosmopolitan**

"Deciding what to save, and periodically deciding what to purge. HOMEFILE®...tells how to systematically store important documents, move records from one file to another and toss dated records."
Andrew Gluck
Worth Magazine

"HOMEFILE® eliminates hours of tedious and frustrating personal filing, and saves money on tax deductions you might have otherwise missed."
Sound Money
The American Public Radio Newsletter

"The Baltimore couple has created a product called HOMEFILE® that can bring order out of the most chaotic mass of paper stuffed inside desk drawers, jammed into overflowing envelopes and hidden in *safe places* all over the house."

Sue Ann Wood
"Dollars and Sense," **St. Louis Post-Dispatch**

"...Can you imagine a world where all your client's deductible receipts are speedily located before April 14—by either the husband or the wife? Idealistic, perhaps, but we think that HOMEFILE® is an ideal idea."

John Freeman Blake, Editor's Message
Tax Management Financial Planning Journal

"...We just did our taxes and it was, well, the word *nightmare* sums it up nicely . . . Next year will be different. We're getting organized. We've discovered HOMEFILE®."

Mary Beth Franklin
St. Petersburg Times

Financial Advantage Series

Life after CDs: A Practical Guide to Safe Investing
J. Michael Martin

Home Filing Made Easy!
Mary E. Martin and J. Michael Martin

Table of Contents

Part I — *Getting Ready To File*

1. Organizing . . . The Key to Financial Success   3

2. Getting Started   13

Part II — *Your File System*

3. The Active Files   25

4. The Quick-Find Index   73

5. The Archives: Near Yet Far

6. Data Collection Center

7. Simple Bill-Paying Routine

Part III — *Related Topics*

8. The Safety Factor and Your Files!   **155**

9. The IRS and Your Files!   **163**

Acknowledgements

We wish to thank the following companies for permission to use their logos:

The American Express® Card Design is a Registered Service Mark of American Express Company. Used by permission. American Express Card Design; Copyright© American Express Company. All rights reserved.

The Discover Card logo is a registered trademark of Novus Credit Services Inc.

MasterCard and the Interlocking Circles are registered marks owned by and used with the permission of MasterCard International Incorporated.

VISA and the Three Bands Design are registered trademarks of Visa International and are reproduced with permission.

Preface

Our years of advising families and small business owners about their finances have confirmed something that we learned raising our own family. . . that good recordkeeping is as difficult as it is essential. After searching in vain through libraries, bookstores, and stationery and office supply stores for a helpful, easy-to-use file system to install at home, all we could find were paragraphs in some home management books and lots of directives to "keep good records" but no real, practical help. So we decided to create a completely new system for our own clients. Every person who heard about the project lit up with enthusiasm and kept asking when it would be available.

As we did more research, we found that the need for a good, practical system was almost universal, cutting across all levels of income, education backgrounds and lifestyles. Encouraged by this insight, we spent two years and more money than we ever intended to make a truly unique personal filing system that is simple to install and easy to maintain: We named our product HOMEFILE®. We were encouraged by its enthusiastic reception; thousands of families and individuals have purchased it and put it into use. Many professional accountants and financial advisers as well as personal finance columnists, authors, radio and TV hosts and magazines have given the HOMEFILE® system glowing reviews and recommendations.

We regularly receive letters from HOMEFILE® users who are thrilled to finally be in control of their papers. One of our favorite letters is from a woman who wrote how nice it is to be able to use her dining room table for entertaining now that her papers are not piled on it! Many happy HOMEFILE® users write that they were delighted to be able to return a defective appliance and get their money back because they knew *exactly* where their receipt was. A frequent comment is, "How much easier it was this year to prepare our income tax return . . . we would never again want to go through tax season without HOMEFILE®."

Now we have packaged the HOMEFILE® system into this convenient book format. We have also included our BILL PAYER™ system of recordkeeping for household bills to make *Home Filing Made Easy!* a truly comprehensive guide to personal and household record organization. (For readers who would enjoy using our colorful, preprinted category divider cards and our Bill Payer caddy with monthly folders, we have included order information at the back of this book.)

This easy-to-use, yet comprehensive system will dramatically lighten your recordkeeping chores, give you more control over your personal affairs, bring you closer to prosperity and provide extra peace of mind as well.

Home Filing Made Easy! is the second in our Financial Advantage series of books designed to break down the challenge of personal financial management into bite-size pieces . . . and to help you master each piece. The first book in the series, *Life after CDs: A Practical Guide to Safe Investing,* is a step-by-step handbook to assist the new investor and retiree in making sound, safe, profitable investment decisions and prosper in a complex financial world.

Introduction

Home filing. How hard can it be? You buy a box of folders at the stationery store, write some labels on the tabs and put them in a drawer, right?

If it's so easy, why does my desktop look like the aftermath of Hurricane Hippo? Why can't I find the kids' Social Security numbers when I need them, and why is the car title in the sock drawer? The furnace went out last night; I know we have a furnace maintenance agreement, but *where* is it?

Sound familiar? Then this book may be just what you need. We wrote *Home Filing Made Easy!* for the millions of people who are tired of saying, "This year I've got to get organized." This handy guidebook will walk you through a step-by-step process for putting all your personal records and important papers in good working order. You will be able to file away any important paper in seconds without wondering where it belongs. Better yet, you'll find it again, effortlessly, when you need it.

Not only will *Home Filing Made Easy!* help you *get organized*; it will help you *stay organized* and serve as a valuable reference resource over the years. In time, you will record in its pages literally thousands of bits of precious data that have never before been brought together in one convenient place. Data that makes it easy to know who to call if you lose your wallet; who to contact with questions about renewals or claims on any of your insurance policies; who are the beneficiaries on any of the IRA or bank accounts you have; a place to list any capital improvements you make on your residence and many other bits and pieces of important data. Your new HOMEFILE® system will simplify your home management paperwork beyond your dreams. You'll wonder how you ever got along without it!

Household bills seem to require a routine that is different from the filing and retrieving of other important papers. Bill paying has a life of its own built around a monthly cycle. *Home Filing Made Easy!* presents an uncomplicated system for paying and keeping track of personal and household bills; this section of the book also provides tips on using credit cards wisely and keeping your checkbook balanced.

If you have a home-based or small business of your own, you are probably keenly aware that your personal records and business records are intimately connected. It is just as important to set up efficient home files as it is to have an organized file system in place for your business or profession.

In our years of experience in the investment field, and especially as family financial advisers, we have learned that *disorganization is a major enemy of personal financial success.* This seems to be equally true across all segments of our population regardless of the levels of formal education or income. Actually, it sometimes seems that those whose income is larger are more vulnerable to this condition because they have enough resources to be a little sloppy with regard to details of good financial accountability, such as balancing checkbooks, responding to auto recalls, taking advantage of product warranties and ignoring extra interest and penalties.

> *"As family financial advisers, we have learned that disorganization is a major enemy of personal financial success. This seems to be true across all segments of our population regardless of the levels of formal education or income."*

Personal disorder not only wastes money and precious time; it is also an *emotional barrier* to success. Being disorganized keeps us from setting clear goals and prevents us from making good decisions. Instead, when we are required to make decisions, we have to make them without adequate information . . . or we avoid making *any* decision, which is a sure way to avoid success even when it is knocking at our door!

So that you can enjoy the financial and emotional benefits of being organized, we present to you *Home Filing Made Easy!* with our sincerest hope that you will use its tested, practical guidance to take control of your records and money and build a solid foundation for your own personal success!

Mike & Mary

Part I

Getting Ready To File

Organizing... The Key to Financial Success

1

Take Charge

Each of us would probably define "success" differently. For one, success may be a financial concept; for another, relationships may be at the heart of it; and for a third, the measure of personal success may be primarily spiritual. Whatever personal success means for you, and likely as not, it is some combination of these, attaining it requires a certain amount of *personal control* over your life. Circumstances and serendipity simply will not conspire to lay personal success at your doorstep. You have to *take charge* to be successful.

Most of us do not live "lives of quiet desperation" as Thoreau suggested. Still, the complexities of daily life in the 1990s do have a way of overwhelming us and sapping our *joie de vivre*. Just to keep a household running smoothly, hold a job, maintain a car, pay taxes and save for retirement can exact every ounce of our energy. Despite all that we have and all that we do, many of us feel like we're on a treadmill, getting nowhere and acccomplishing nothing.

The human race has long desired the amenities that modern civilization affords us. Just think for a moment how rich we are in the way of educational opportunities, insurance protection, personal transportation, labor-saving appliances, recreational choices, government services, advanced healthcare, a chance to retire and so many other advantages. We ought to be having the time of our lives. Sometimes, though, each of these benefits of civilization seems to shackle us to another five pounds of paper. After a while, we have so many benefits we can barely move!

As we prepare to usher in the 21st century, staying on top of our daily affairs and feeling in control may seem to be an unattainable dream. That was certainly true for *our* household before we developed the HOMEFILE® system. We used to say, "If *we* can't stay on top of things with the benefits of our degrees in law and accounting and our years of financial experience, how in the world can people without specialized training ever cope?" The more families we met in our financial planning practice, the more we were convinced that most of us moderns need a way to organize our personal records to save us time and money and to give us a sense of being in charge again. Are we overstating the problem? No, we don't think so.

Why Good Recordkeeping Is So Vital

According to the International Board of Certified Financial Planners (IBCFP) in Denver, Colorado, planning our personal finances involves six major areas:

1. Cash flow
2. Risk management
3. Tax planning
4. Investment planning
5. Retirement planning
6. Estate planning

How we spend our money, whether our savings are productive, building our family's financial security—these are the bedrock issues of our financial lives. Not only that, but if we let them get out of control, they produce anxiety that can easily derail us from pursuing the other things in our lives that are even more important to us.

Our professional experience convinces us that *personal financial disorganization* is one of the most common, serious obstacles to personal success in life. For most of us, the ability to make better financial decisions would seem to be a sufficient motivation to set up a good filing system at home, but the benefits of being organized actually go much deeper to issues such as self-esteem and a feeling of progress. Perhaps that is why a first-ever Gallup poll about New Year's resolutions in 1991 found that 16% of Americans listed as their number one resolution, "This year I have to get my finances organized." The only resolution that ranked higher (17%) was losing weight!

To really take charge of those six areas of personal finance, you need access to current information about your personal affairs—a comprehensive set of records about your spending, investments, insurance, taxes, etc. As with anything else in life that is worthwhile, having a set of good working files takes just two things: a little knowledge and a little initiative. Below is a brief survey of the issues involved in these six areas of your life to give you a sense of the importance of keeping your affairs in order and to motivate you to take the initiative. *Home Filing Made Easy!* will give you the knowledge and confidence to make your home filing system work for you!

Cash Flow

Most of us work hard to earn money so we can exchange it for goods and services that we need or want. We also try, sometimes with mixed success, to save part of what we earn for unexpected future expenses or to provide for our needs when we are older. In our finer moments, we may even be inclined to give away some of our money to benefit others.

Cash is a limited resource; most of us cannot afford to buy everything that strikes our fancy, give away as much as we want to or have as big a nest egg as we would prefer. This being so, we make choices; we allocate our cash, either by design or by default, to some combination of spending, taxes, saving and gifting.

How one person spends his or her cash can be very similar to the way the next door neighbor does . . . or it might be radically different! We have some very prosperous clients who wouldn't dream of buying a brand-new car, and a few considerably less well-heeled who would feel shabby if their vehicle were more than 3 years old. We all have different needs, wants and personalities. The differences are often reflected in how we decide to allocate our money.

We use the expression, "Time is money." Underlying this idiom is the reality that money is just a social convention that allows citizens to exchange their work (time) for that of others. So how we spend our money is really the story of how we spend our most precious resource, our time. We spend it on what is most important to us. Or do we?

Spending Plan. Serving as advisers to hundreds of people, we have learned that few, very few, actually have a written household budget. Only about half of all households have a fairly accurate sense of how their cash is allocated. The other half, not having very much information about where they have been spending their income, feel very dissatisfied with their use of money. Often these are the people who experience the most anxiety about money. They usually write checks for whatever seems most pressing or important at the moment. Over the course of a year, they make thousands of decisions but not with full knowledge of the consequences and not in the context of a plan to achieve what they really want.

The surest way to increase our sense of financial well-being and to take charge of how our money is allocated is to write down a spending plan. We used to call it a *budget*, but a *spending plan* sounds a lot more pleasant!

The starting point for making a spending plan is to list those things that cost money that are really important to us. The next step is to see how we have *actually* been spending our money and compare it with how we *want* to spend it. To do this, we need—you guessed it—*information*. That, of course, is where recordkeeping comes in.

Bill-Paying. We have intentionally not provided a filing category in the HOMEFILE® system for bills because, as we said in the introduction, bill-paying has a life of its own, built more or less around a monthly cycle, and it cries out for a separate strategy. So we developed a separate bill-paying system. In Chapter 7, you will learn how to set up a bill-paying system that will help you track your household outlays and see exactly how you are presently spending your money. Then you will be in a position to set your priorities and derive more satisfaction from your spending.

Risk Management

Decisions about insurance are among the most difficult; they involve allocating part of our limited cash flow to protect ourselves against a future event that probably will not occur. Most of us prefer to imagine that we will not be the victims of costly illnesses, huge lawsuits, tragic loss of property or premature death; hence, we are not eager to spend our earnings to protect ourselves and our families from such unlikely losses. That is why the adage endures, "Insurance is sold, not bought."

In its zeal to protect us, the insurance industry has become possibly the largest generator of printed materials in the whole economy. Unfortunately, we need to retain much of what the industry generates! The HOMEFILE® system devotes four of its 22 filing categories to insurance.

You will find that it is extremely helpful to segregate your insurance documents by type: auto, health, life and property. Separating them makes it easier to put away policies, receipts and claims documents; more importantly, you'll find it much simpler to locate information when you have a claim or want to compare your policy terms with another that is available.

Tax Planning

Fear can be a great motivator! If the prospect of making better financial decisions or feeling that we have control over our lives does not spark our interest in organizing our papers, the fear of an IRS audit often does the trick. When we make guest appearances on radio and TV talk shows, we get more questions about the government's requirements for recordkeeping than anything else, and understandably so.

The tax code has some pretty outrageous rules about saving documentation for the income and deductions claimed on our tax returns. To be absolutely sure about some particular feature, you may want to consult a tax authority. For most situations, though, the HOMEFILE® system provides clear recordkeeping guidelines. You will find this information (see

Chapter 3) in the category descriptions under the heading, "When To Remove." The "Taxes (Income)" category description also refers you to numerous free IRS publications that give detailed advice on record requirements.

The rule of thumb is that the IRS may require you to present supporting documentation for up to three years after a return is filed for any reason at all—or no reason at all! The time limit extends to six years if there is reason to suspect that you have significantly underreported your income, and there is no time limit at all for cases of fraud. Most tax advisers recommend keeping tax returns and supporting documents for six years. In Chapter 9, we point out some kinds of records that you will want to hang onto indefinitely.

Finally, in the file labeled "Taxes (Income)," you should keep only the prior year's tax return with its supporting paperwork and a few other items that are listed in the category description for "Taxes (Income)." If you kept in that file everything that had any tax consequence (mortgage papers, charitable contributions, medical bills, etc.), approximately half of all your papers would be crammed into the Tax file! It's much more efficient to keep things filed in their own category all year so you can find them when you need them for nontax reasons.

Investment Planning

Investment files are among the most complicated; they can also be among the most frequently accessed, so keeping them in order can take a lot of stress out of your life. To simplify the recordkeeping, HOMEFILE® distinguishes between "Retirement Savings," which are tax-deferred, and "Investments," which refers to your regular, taxable investments, such as stocks, bonds and mutual funds. Two other categories of investment are "Real Estate," which has its own file, and "Annuities," which is included in the "Life Insurance and Annuities" category.

Can you imagine what it would be like if you had to wade through your mutual fund and brokerage statements to find the property tax records for the ocean condo you bought as an investment? These investment category separations work very smoothly and efficiently. Just pay attention to the category descriptions, or use the Quick-Find Index in Chapter 4; in no time at all, you will be so used to them that you will file and find investment records without looking them up.

Retirement Planning

For many American households, building a retirement nest egg is their most important savings goal. Because retirement saving is so vital, people want frequent access to information about their IRAs, Keoghs, SEPs, 401(k)s and other tax-deferred accounts. They want to see how their accounts are progressing and compare their investment results and terms with alternative tax-advantaged investments they may be considering.

The HOMEFILE® system makes a distinction between the self-administered retirement savings (such as IRAs) and the retirement plans or accounts that people have where they work. Statements for the latter are kept in the file called "Employment" because increasingly employees are presented with a menu of benefit selections that can be traded off or substituted for one another. Because these benefits are so intertwined with employment decisions, it works better to keep all employee benefit records, even retirement accounts, together in one place. After you retire, we recommend moving these records to the "Retirement Savings" file.

Estate Planning

We have often helped surviving family members sort through the files of a departed parent or spouse to prepare for estate settlement and final tax accounting. One client's husband had mixed household and business records for 20 years; separating them was for her tedious and frustrating to the point of tears. We can assure you from our experience that orderly records are a deeply appreciated gift to the family, both emotionally and financially.

Tax and estate regulations have enormously complicated the lot of our survivors after our departure from this planet! Using the HOMEFILE® system, a great personal advantage in our own lives, reduces stress and uncertainty for those we love after we are gone. Wills and trust documents are easily found because their location is recorded on the form in Chapter 6.

Information on investments, real property, insurance, retirement accounts and employee benefits are all readily accessible. In the absence of orderly records, estate settlement is complicated and takes longer, insurance policies and other assets are often missed entirely, professional expenses soar, family rela-

Organized for Success

tionships are stressed and the estate tax bill can skyrocket. We've seen order and we've seen disorder—order is better!

A wealth of "success literature" is available to us today. Motivational writers such as Og Mandino, Ken Blanchard, Norman Vincent Peale, Zig Ziglar, Lou Tice and many others stir our souls and teach us to set personal goals and persevere toward achieving them. We read these authors as often as we can and highly recommend them to anyone who will listen. In our own humble way, we have written *Home Filing Made Easy!* as a practical complement to that helpful body of literature.

It is extremely important and valuable for you to set lofty goals for prosperity, learning, health, generosity, spiritual growth and a happy home life. Yet, if you set out to achieve these while neglecting the foundations of personal organization, you will be headed only for frustration. If you set admirable goals and have the finest intentions but your daily routine, thoughts and habits are disorderly, you will find yourself riddled with anxiety and frozen into indecision, unable to move ahead.

Trying to cope with disorganized personal files in today's complex society is like driving down the interstate at rush hour in an ox-drawn wagon; you can't keep up with the traffic, and you'll constantly be afraid of being run over by events. So we invite you to organize for success. Hop into the driver's seat of HOMEFILE®, the limousine of personal organization systems, and enjoy the ride . . . and your life!

New Beginning

Because we have to keep accessible so many types of essential documents, it's easy to see why filing is so complicated. The simple act of putting something away so it can be found again requires a complex decision process. What do I call it? What file should it go in? Will I remember where I put it? Could someone else find it? Should I make a new file? Is there a tax reason to keep this, or can I just toss it? Oh, look at these old records; I don't need them . . . *or do I?*

You may have conducted frustrating forays into piles of paper on your desk or in a closet searching for a warranty or a tax return. Your medical receipts and bank statements may have been mixed together in a drawer or in the dining room hutch. You might have stood in line for an hour at the Department of Motor Vehicles trying to replace the lost title for the car you are selling. Believe us, you are not alone! In our experience, only 10 percent to 15 percent of all households really have their records under control.

You are holding in your hands a personal filing system that, with a little effort on your part, will relegate your filing blues to the distant past. Our staff took two years to research, design and write the system, but you'll be able to put it to work in a couple hours . . . and it will serve you and your household for many years to come!

- No more indecision about where to file a document!
- No more frustrating searches for missing papers!
- No more lost warranties and missed tax deductions!
- No more fears of an IRS audit!

The HOMEFILE® system consists of 22 categories for your *active* files and 10 parallel categories for your *archive* files; these will accommodate the whole range of your paper records in good, clear order. In Chapter 3, you will find a two-page *category description* for each active file category. These descriptions indicate exactly which items you need to keep in each file. They also point out clearly when you may remove items either to the trash (or recycling bin) or to your archive area for long-term storage.

> *"You will be able to put this system to work in a couple hours . . . and it will serve you and your household for many years to come!"*

These category descriptions even tell you what doesn't belong in the file that you might be inclined to put there. After all, the choices and possibilities are numerous. For example, should your mortgage records be filed under "Bank Accounts," "Credit" or "Residence"? For all these potentially ambiguous situations, we have simplified your life by selecting one file that you can use consistently. The result is a filing *standard* that makes it possible for you, your spouse or anyone with whom you share the files to put away and retrieve papers without a hitch.

We hope that you are eager to get started. In Chapter 2, we break down the personal filing routine into four simple steps. Then we'll give you some working tips on selecting filing containers and supplies.

Getting Started

Supplies

The HOMEFILE® system consists of 22 file categories for your *active* files and ten for your *archives* (things that you need to keep for a long time but rarely have to access). To get your system in place, you need only the following supplies:

- 1 copy of *Home Filing Made Easy!*
- 33 hanging file folders with labels
- 1 box of manila folders
- 1 felt-tipped marker
- Appropriate file cabinet or box
- Important papers looking for a neat home!

Hanging files. These files have a metal or plastic hook extending from the upper corners. When they are inserted into a file drawer, the folders are suspended from rails on both sides of the drawer, making it easy to push them aside to add more files. (Not every file cabinet or file box is designed to accommodate hanging files . . . more about that later.) For your principal file categories, hanging files are vastly superior to plain manila folders. They never slide one under the other; instead, they remain upright in the drawer because they are suspended from the top edge. They are also larger than manila folders so they can hold more papers.

Most people prefer standard-sized hanging files because they use less space than legal files and they easily accommodate virtually any document. Many real estate closing documents still come on legal size paper, but these can be folded in half to fit a standard file. We are finding that even the legal profession is moving toward standard 8 ½ x 11-inch paper! (If you still prefer the roominess of wide files, hanging legal files are readily available.) Stationery and office supply stores and most "warehouse" and "membership" stores carry a wide selection of file folders. To give your personal files a professional flair and make them inviting to use, you might want to spend a little extra money to buy them in a bright color; you could even have different colors for active files and archives. Colored hanging files cost from $7 to $14 for a box of 25, while the no-frills, army-green kind runs about $4 to $8 a box.

Manila folders.   These are very inexpensive; a box of 100 costs from $4 to $7. You will probably use a lot of these over the years, so buy a whole box and keep a supply handy. Manila folders are used to subdivide your main filing categories. For example, in your bank account file you will want to segregate documents from the different banks that you deal with. Label one manila folder for each bank, and keep them in the hanging file marked "Bank Accounts." The category descriptions in Chapter 3 tell you where manila folders can be useful. Some folders come in bright colors, which could be helpful as well as attractive.

Pens and labels.   To mark file labels so that you can read them easily, you need a thin-line marker or felt-tipped pen in a dark color. Your files will be especially impressive if you use one color ink for hanging file labels and a second color to label the manila folders!

File Cabinets

File cabinets or file containers are available in such a great range of sizes, features and prices that you may appreciate some additional information to help you select just the right one to meet your needs. If you have already picked out your file container, you may want to skip to the next section on "Preparing Your Files."

File cabinets range from gray-metal functional to fine cabinetry. They can be locking or nonlocking, and they can be equipped for hanging files or not. Cabinets may have from one to five drawers, be vertical or lateral and be constructed solidly or inexpensively. You can, of course, find file cabinets in office supply outlets. You can also find some good bargains from classified ads, yard sales, swap meets and relatives!

Size. As you try to determine the optimum combination of features and price, you may want to consider *size* first. The number of file drawers you need depends on factors such as family size, number of family members employed, how many cars you keep records for, insurance policies, residences, investments, etc. One good clue is how much space your current files take. If you are unsure about the size you need, our recommendation is to err on the side of *large*. It is difficult for most people to prune their personal files down to lean, mean fighting trim. If you have enough drawer capacity from the start, you'll have the luxury of holding onto stuff you'd rather not toss . . . just yet! Most households can run smoothly with two file drawers for current files and another two for archives.

One of the beauties of the HOMEFILE® system is that it will grow with you. You will *never* again have to start all over with a new system. You can always add more hanging files and folders for additional cars, more household members, more policies and more investments. Your 22 categories will always be appropriate, and your Quick-Find Index will always work!

Hanging file rails. One file cabinet feature you don't want to skimp on is the ability to accommodate hanging files. Rails for hanging files can be built into the file, or there may be slots in the rear of the drawer to hold in place rails that you purchase separately. It is best to buy a file with the rails already built in because they are the sturdiest. The next most effective are the file cabinets that have slots built in to hold the braces for the hanging files that you will insert. Lastly, some cabinets have neither. For these you can purchase hanging file rail kits that can be cut to proper size, assembled and then placed in the drawers. They are fairly inexpensive and easy to assemble. The rails are scored and can be bent off with pliers at the desired size. This makes a workable solution for an unusual type of container or furniture, such as an antique desk that you want to use for your files.

Vertical and lateral files.   The most common configuration for a file cabinet is called a *vertical file*, in which the files are arranged from front to back in the drawer. Another arrangement, called a *lateral file,* requires a wider cabinet; when the drawer is opened, it displays files arranged from left to right. A lateral file may fit into a space that would be impractical for a vertical file, for example, in a narrow area or near a door that might be impeded by pulling out a long drawer. Deciding where you will keep your files will help you determine which configuration is best for you. Incidentally, vertical files are usually less expensive.

Wood or metal.   While you are mentally arranging your furniture, this may be a good time to compare the appropriateness of a wood cabinet versus a standard metal one. From a practical standpoint, you will be more likely to use your file regularly if it is in a convenient place. If being convenient means that you will locate your files where they will be on display in your home, you may want to consider them as furniture. Check the "Source Guide" at the end of the book for some manufacturers who produce fine file cabinets. They offer a wide range of styles, for example, a lovely Queen Ann two-drawer unit, handsome yet sturdy one- and two-drawer file cabinet end tables and free-standing oak file cabinets. Providing an attractive as well as functional setting for your files makes it much more likely that you will use them and actually enjoy the time you spend filing and organizing.

Full suspension.   This is a major feature you should be aware of when looking for filing cabinets. Suspension has to do with being able to roll out the file drawer to the full length of the drawer. It allows you to reach the folders in the rear of the file drawer. Some of the cheaper models that you may be tempted to buy will cause you frustration over the years as you experience the inconvenience of not being able to reach the files in the back of the drawer. Being able to reach never looks like a problem when the cabinet is empty; it becomes much more apparent when the drawer is full.

You can usually avoid the cabinet's tipping over by never opening more than one drawer at a time. Most of the good cabinets have a locking device on them that won't allow you to open more than one drawer at a time. Ask the salesperson to demonstrate these features. You want to be sure that you know what you are getting. Remember that this filing cabinet is an investment meant to serve you for years to come.

Alternative file containers.   At the other end of the cost spectrum are some really creative, inexpensive filing containers; you will see them lining the aisle of the *office supply super stores*. At prices ranging from $5 to $25, you can choose from sturdy cardboard storage boxes, rugged plastic "crates" and an array of other innovative portable filing containers. Again we urge you to select ones that will hold your hanging files. Some in this price range do, but many do not.

The smaller containers are great for college students and people striking out on their own, who may not have lots of room or a budget to buy a full-standing file cabinet. They are just beginning to accumulate papers from vehicles, apartments, insurance policies and credit cards. As a matter of fact, you might consider making a gift of *Home Filing Made Easy!* to those friends and family members who are starting out. Helping them to create good habits of personal organization is a gift to benefit them for a *lifetime*.

Uses for parallel sets of files.   Two other practical uses of the smaller filing containers are worth commenting on. Lots of people are away from home for long stretches of time, most of them living in RVs or vacation homes. In these situations, it is a great idea to set up a parallel set of files to keep track of the important stuff while you are away. Then it's a snap to pop papers into the permanent files when you get back. Parallel files can also be used effectively when caring for an aging parent's paperwork. By having a small, portable file system for this use, you can take care of Mom's or Dad's files wherever it is most convenient for you.

Innovative ideas.   Finally, from our neighbors and customers, here are a few innovative ideas for setting up your files in a living room, bedroom or family room. Shop around at garage sales for a two-drawer file cabinet. Households move up or down in size, and you will often find good two-drawer models at these sales. Cut a circle of plywood large enough to extend beyond the ends of the file cabinet. Purchase or make a fabric tablecloth to match the room's decor, and drape it over the plywood covering the cabinet. As an option, you could have a glass circle made at a glass shop (about $15 to $30). The glass can be placed on top of the decorative fabric. This is an attractive way to bring your files right into your living areas and maintain them in a private yet convenient place.

Another innovative idea comes from our neighbor, Barbara. At a local chain store, she recently purchased a desktop that fits over a two-drawer file cabinet and becomes a nice, roomy desk when extended. When not in use as a desk, the legs fold up, and the desktop, which is hinged, folds down and out of the way, leaving the file cabinet accessible and freeing floor space for other activities.

Here is another idea for those who have many papers to file and are looking for an economical solution. Place two 2-drawer file cabinets about four feet apart and lay a flat door across them. If you don't happen to have an extra door around, try a lumber supply place for an unfinished hollow door, or have a sheet of plywood cut to fit your space. A little paint, stain or even some Contact™ paper would give your desk a nice appearance. This is an inexpensive way to acquire a huge desk with four file drawers.

Safe-Deposit Box/ Fireproof Files

Some of your papers would be difficult or impossible to replace; old family records and court orders fall in this category. To give valuable documents the highest possible level of protection against loss by fire or theft, you may want to rent a safe-deposit box at a convenient bank. See Chapter 6 for a representative list of such documents, and ask your legal or financial advisers for their insights. Box rental fees, starting at $20, may be tax deductible; check with your tax return preparer or your tax manual.

If the cost or inconvenience of a bank box is objectionable, another option is to acquire a fireproof container to keep at home. These containers range from small portable boxes to large fireproof safes and even four-drawer fireproof file cabinets selling for a few hundred dollars. See the "Source Guide" for the names of some manufacturers.

If you keep documents or other valuables in a safe-deposit box or fireproof container separate from your regular files, it is a good idea to keep in the regular files a photocopy of the document, a list of their locations and possibly a list of their contents. *Home Filing Made Easy!* has a form for that purpose in Chapter 6.

Preparing Your Files

Once you have decided upon and secured your file cabinet(s) and supplies, you are ready to begin. To take full advantage of the complete HOMEFILE® system, you need a total of 33 hanging files: 23 for your active files and 10 for your archives.

Step 1
Hanging the Files

Place 23 hanging files in the file drawer or container where your active records will be stored—one hanging file for each of the 22 categories and one to store *Home Filing Made Easy!*, which includes the *Quick-Find Index* to your new files. The remaining 10 hanging files are for long-term storage—your archives. Since you probably won't need frequent access to your archives, they can be kept in a more remote place in your home if filing space is at a premium. Be sure to keep them high and dry!

Step 2
Labeling the
Active Categories

Turn to Chapter 3, where you will find an alphabetical list of the active file categories. Using your felt-tipped pen and the tabs that come with your hanging files, label each folder with one of the active category titles. Begin with "Autos" at the front of the drawer or box, and work toward the back. If you have a lateral file, you will probably be most comfortable working from right to left. If you will usually be accessing your files from your desk chair, have the file labels face the chair. Make a label marked "Handbook & Index" for the first hanging file in the drawer, and use it to store this book. Flag the *Quick-Find Index* so you can find it quickly.

In Chapter 3, you will also find a detailed description of everything that belongs in each file category. If you would like the luxury of having this information right in each file for easy reference—and would prefer not to write all these file labels—you can buy colorful, plastic-tabbed category cards preprinted with the category titles and all the information detailing what to file and not file under each category and how long you need to save the information. You can find an order form for this complete HOMEFILE® Organizer Kit in the back of this book.

Step 3
Labeling the
Archive Categories

Archive files hold those tax-related and personal documents that you want to keep for a long, long time. Having separate files for long-term storage prevents your active files from getting congested with noncurrent papers. The category descriptions found in Chapter 3 tell you when to move papers to your archives. Chapter 4 gives you more information about the archives. The ten archive categories parallel ten of the active ones. Turn to Chapter 4 and label each of the ten archive hanging files with one of the archive categories listed there.

Step 4
Inserting
Manila Folders

You will find that you use some of your active categories more often than others. Files such as "Autos," "Bank Accounts," "Investments," "Medical Records" and "Personal" will probably work best if you put manila folders in them to subdivide the major categories. For example, you can establish separate manila folders for different bank accounts, cars, family members; and don't forget a "pet" folder for Fido or Kitty! When labeling these folders, write with a dark pen or marker that will be easy to read.

You're Ready To File!

Now you have all the files that you'll need to house your important papers and make them easily accessible. Getting everything *into* these files involves two stages: filing *new* stuff and filing *old* stuff.

Filing *New* Papers and Documents

Filing new papers as they arrive in the mail is the easiest part, taking almost no effort and just the tiniest bit of discipline. Each time you have something new to file away, simply open *Home Filing Made Easy!* to the *Quick-Find Index* in Chapter 4. Look up the item by name on the index, and put it in the category file that it tells you. That's it! To find it again, use the same procedure.

As your mail arrives each day, separate the bills and any important papers you want to keep in your files from the catalogs and other mail. Put those bills where you are keeping your "bills to pay" (see Chapter 7, "Simple Bill-Paying Routine"). Put your "to file" items in your "to file" bin or directly into their proper files. If you have any questions concerning that category after checking the Quick-Find Index, look up the complete category description in Chapter 3 and read it over. As you work this routine a few times, you will become so familiar with the HOMEFILE® system that you'll soon be doing it without effort.

Organizing *Accumulated* Records

If you've been moving down the road of life for more than a few years, chances are that putting order into your accumulated pile of important papers involves a little more time and effort at first. If you have paper collections randomly stashed all over your house, be assured that you are not alone! The task of organizing everything may not be as monumental as it may at first appear. You are less likely to be overwhelmed—and more likely to complete the task—if you take the "divide and conquer" approach. That is, tackle each drawerful or pile one at a time.

First, scan the items in the pile for any common characteristics. Are there lots of medical papers, for example, or auto-related or insurance material? If so, turn to the appropriate category description in Chapter 3, and read it over to familiarize yourself with the guidelines. Now pick up one paper at a time and, using the information from the category description, decide to do one of three things with each document:

1. PLACE it in the appropriate active file if it is something that belongs in your current files *or*

2. PLACE it in the appropriate archive file if it needs to be kept for a long time but you are unlikely to need it in the next year *or*

3. DISPOSE of it if you truly don't need it at all. See the "When To Remove" section of the appropriate category description.

Time for a break? You've already come a long way. You deserve a rest; why not store *Home Filing Made Easy!* in the file you labeled, "Handbook and Index"? When you return, you can turn to Chapter 3 and learn how to use the active files.

Part II

Your File System

Part II
Part II

Part II
Part II
Part II
Part II
Part II
Part II

The Active Files

About the Category Descriptions. The category descriptions in this chapter are the heart of your file reference system. They are listed in alphabetical order by category. Each category description spells out exactly what kinds of papers belong under that category. It even gives you guidance on cleaning out that file by explaining how long you need to retain different documents.

How To Use
the Category Descriptions

The category descriptions are packed with valuable information, yet they are remarkably easy to use. Each one has the same following basic three-section format:

FILE HERE. This section lists specific papers and documents that ought to be stored in this category. When deciding where to file a particular document, look here first.

DO NOT FILE HERE. Here, HOMEFILE® refers you to other file categories that may be more appropriate for the item you want to store. Sometimes you will have an intuitive impression of the right category for a document, but the HOMEFILE® system may direct it to another file that is more appropriate.

The "Do Not File Here" section of each category description provides a cross-reference, making it easy to find the *proper* category for the item. For example, the "Do Not File Here" section of the "Auto" category description says: "Do not file auto insurance papers here; they belong in the 'Insurance: (Auto)' file."

WHEN TO REMOVE. When you feel inspired to purge your current files (or when your files have become too crowded to fit one more document), read the "When To Remove" section of the category in question. We have tried to take the trauma out of pruning your files by pointing out criteria for saving or disposing of various kinds of documents.

There are 22 *active* category descriptions. There are also 10 *archive* category descriptions... more about these in Chapter 4. The active categories are as follows:

File Categories

AUTOS, BOATS & RVs
BANK ACCOUNTS
CHARITIES
CREDIT
EMPLOYMENT
EXPENSES (Employment & "Misc.")
INSURANCE (Autos, Boats & RVs)
INSURANCE (Health & Disability)
INSURANCE (Home & Property)
INSURANCE (Life & Annuity)
INVESTMENTS
MEDICAL RECORDS
PERSONAL
REAL ESTATE
RESIDENCE
RETIREMENT SAVINGS
SCHOOLS & CHILDCARE
SELF-EMPLOYED
SOCIAL SECURITY
TAXES (INCOME)
WARRANTIES & RECEIPTS
WILLS & TRUSTS

Helpful Suggestions

Photocopies. Sometimes it is important to treat originals and photocopies differently in your filing system. This is made clear throughout the series of category descriptions. The words *copies or photocopies* are italicized for emphasis when this distinction is significant.

Additional information. Some category descriptions provide additional information or guidance that is appropriate to that particular file. For example, some descriptions suggest that you create separate manila folders to divide papers within that file category. This instruction appears at the top of the "File Here" section.

Free information. Several category descriptions indicate where you can obtain free information about the tax aspects of items in that file. These always appear inside a box labeled "Helpful Materials."

Additional notes. A number of category descriptions have additional "notes" that provide helpful instructions specifically related to their particular file categories. For example, the "Wills & Trusts" description notes that an original will should not be stored in a safe-deposit box at a bank because in many states the box could be sealed upon notification to the bank of the owner's death; the information about the owner's last wishes would not be available to the family when they most needed it!

Here is the best way to familiarize yourself with all these tips: The first few times you file something in a particular category, scan its category description to become familiar with its guidance. You will be surprised how quickly and effortlessly you will become expert at using the HOMEFILE® system this way. And if you forget anything, the category description is always right in the book in your front file for handy reference!

DO NOT FILE HERE

- Accident Records
    - *See:* **INSURANCE (AUTO)**

- Auto Insurance Information
    - *See:* **INSURANCE (AUTO)**

- Records of Auto Use for Business or Healthcare
    - *See:* **EXPENSES (EMPLOYMENT & "MISC.")**
    - **MEDICAL RECORDS**
    - **SELF-EMPLOYED**

WHEN TO REMOVE

When You No Longer Own the Vehicle

- Your transfer of title and license plate transfer records may be kept, but all other papers may be disposed of unless any legal claims are pending.

MAKE A SEPARATE MANILA FOLDER FOR EACH VEHICLE.

- List of All:
  - Autos
  - Boats
  - Recreational vehicles
  - Heavy equipment

  Include: {
  - Make & model
  - Year (note new/used)
  - ID number
  - Seller's name
  - Purchase date

- Correspondence Related to Vehicles

- Inspection Records

- Oil Change and Maintenance Records (Include date and mileage.)

- Papers from Dealer, *Including:*
  - Warranties
  - User manuals
  - Manufacturer's recall information

- *Photocopy* of Registration

- Purchase Warranties

- Receipts For:
  - Repairs
  - Tires, batteries and parts
  - (On each receipt, write date and mileage.)

- Title Record *Copies* (Keep *originals* in safe-deposit or fireproof box.)

- Traffic or Parking Ticket Information
  - Date to write for expungement if necessary.

AUTOS
BOATS & RVs

DO NOT FILE HERE

- CDs and IRAs
  - *See:* **INVESTMENTS** or **RETIREMENT SAVINGS**

- Credit Card Records
  - *See:* **CREDIT**

- Loan Records
  - *See:* **CREDIT**

- Mortgage Information
  - *See:* **RESIDENCE** or **REAL ESTATE**

WHEN TO REMOVE

- Checkbook Register
  - Should be dated and stored with old checks.

- Checks
  - After one year, you may dispose of nontax-related checks, or put them away in a check-saving box.
  - After preparing taxes, keep all tax-related checks with your copy of tax return.
    - *See:* **Chapter 9,** "The IRS and Your Files," for more information.

- Deposit Slips
  - May be kept for 6 years as some evidence of the source of funds deposited (Write the source on back of the slip.)

- Monthly Statements
  - May be disposed of after each year's taxes have been prepared.

- Withdrawal and Transfer Slips
  - May ordinarily be disposed of after these transactions appear correctly on a monthly statement.

BANK ACCOUNTS

MAKE A SEPARATE MANILA FOLDER FOR EACH BANK.

- Code for Automated Teller Machine (ATM) Bank Cards, Including Personal Identification Numbers (PIN)and Account Numbers (or keep in a locked safe.)

- Credit Union Statements
  – Except loan statements
    See: **CREDIT**

- Deposit, Withdrawal and Transfer Slips

- Duplicate Bank Cards for ATMs

- Latest Month's Canceled Checks
    See: **Chapter 7,** "Simple Bill-Paying Routine"

- Monthly Checking Account Statements

- Savings Account Statements and Passbooks

- 1099 Forms from Banks

Note: *Each month after reconciling statements, put tax-related canceled checks into the appropriate files such as "Expenses," "Medical Records," "Charities," etc. Put the rest of your canceled checks in a separate box used just for storing checks.*

BANK ACCOUNTS

DO NOT FILE HERE

- Contributions That Are Not Tax Deductible (Check the tax status of any "charities" you are unsure of.)
    - *See:* "Source Guide" at the end of *Home Filing Made Easy!*

- Political Contributions
    - *See:* **PERSONAL**

WHEN TO REMOVE

- Once a Year
  - Prune this file by removing outdated or unwanted solicitations.

- Tax-Related Records
  - Should be kept for 3–6 years. After each year's tax return has been filed, keep the appropriate contribution records with a copy of that tax return in:
    - **TAXES (INCOME)**

CHARITIES

- Appraisal Statements Concerning Donated Property

- Church Envelopes

- Letters from Charities Acknowledging Value of Gifts

- List of Favorite Charities, *Including:*
    Addresses
    Phone numbers
    Contact persons

- Log of Mileage Expenses Incurred for Volunteer Work

- Pledges and Information Concerning Any Outstanding Pledges

- Receipts and/or Canceled Checks for All Cash Contributions to Tax-Exempt Organizations
  – Take contributions checks from among those returned by your bank each month after you reconcile your bank account.

- Receipts for Noncash Donations of Items, *Including:*
    Clothing and household goods to Salvation Army, etc.

- Solicitations, Brochures, Etc. for Possible Later Response

CHARITIES

DO NOT FILE HERE

- Checking and Savings Account Information
  - *See:* **BANK ACCOUNTS**

- Loan Payment Books
  - You may prefer to keep these with your current bills.

- Mortgage Information
  - *See:* **RESIDENCE** or **REAL ESTATE**

- Papers Regarding Loans You Have Made to Others
  - *See:* **INVESTMENTS**

- Purchase Receipts Regarding Business Expenses
  - *See:* **EXPENSES** or **SELF-EMPLOYED**

WHEN TO REMOVE

- Canceled Checks or Drafts
  - Can be disposed of when they are one year old unless they are tax-related, in which case you should keep them with your tax return.

- Credit Purchase Receipts
  - May be discarded after appearing on credit card statement *and* when not needed for warranties, merchandise returns or taxes.

- Loan Payment Receipts
  - May be disposed of when a loan is paid in full.
  - You may keep canceled notes in
    ARCHIVE: CREDIT for 2 years.

- Monthly Statements
  - May be discarded after each year's tax return is filed unless needed for long-term tax records.

CREDIT

FILE HERE

MAKE A SEPARATE MANILA FOLDER FOR EACH CREDIT RELATIONSHIP.

- Bank Loan Applications

- Credit Card Information, *Including:*
  - Code numbers
  - Phone numbers for lost cards and for inquiries
  - Duplicate cards
  - List of all credit cards and numbers
  - Purchase receipts
  - Monthly statements (after making monthly payments)
  - Checks or drafts from credit card accounts, *including:*
    - Canceled checks
    - Unused checks

- Credit Reports

- Correspondence with Credit Agencies

- Papers Regarding Bank Loans Outstanding and Loans Paid

- Personal Financial Statement (Balance Sheet)

- Receipts for Loan Payments Made

- Records Related to Deductibility of Interest Payments

- Tuition Loan Documents

CREDIT

DO NOT FILE HERE

- Job-Related Expenses
    - Such as professional fees, travel expenses.
        See: **EXPENSES (EMPLOYMENT & "MISC.")**

- Medical Insurance Records
        See: **INSURANCE (HEALTH & DISABILITY)**

- Pension Income Records
        See: **RETIREMENT SAVINGS** or **SOCIAL SECURITY**

- 1099s from Investments or Banks
        See: **BANK ACCOUNTS** or **INVESTMENTS**

WHEN TO REMOVE

- At Year's End
    - Discard all but the final, cumulative pay stubs for the year.

- After Each Year's Tax Filing
    - Move that calendar year's employment records to:
        ARCHIVE: EMPLOYMENT
    - Keep old employment records there until benefits no longer apply (which may mean into your retirement years).

MAKE A SEPARATE MANILA FOLDER FOR EACH WORKING FAMILY MEMBER.

- Employee Benefits Descriptions

- Employee Handbook

- Employer's Name, Address and Phone Number

- Independent Contractor's 1099s

- Papers Regarding
    Stock options
    Retirement plans
    Deferred compensation agreements [e.g., 401(k)]
    Profit-sharing accounts
    Other employee benefits

- Paycheck Stub
  – Most recent one from each employer

- Resume

- Unemployment Compensation Records

- W-2s

While You Are Still Working
- Keep pension, profit-sharing and other employment-related retirement benefits in this file.

Once You Retire and Begin Receiving Pension Income
- Keep pension-related records in:
    RETIREMENT SAVINGS

EMPLOYMENT

DO NOT FILE HERE

- Records of a Business
  - This file is only for records of *personal outlays* for business or income-producing purposes, especially those incurred as an employee, which might be fully or partially deductible from your personal taxable income.

- Regular Household Bills
    See: **Chapter 7,** "Simple Bill-Paying Routine"

Note: There is a separate file labeled **SELF-EMPLOYED,** *which is appropriate for filing some materials related to your own small business enterprise.*

WHEN TO REMOVE

- Tax-Related Records
  - Should be kept for 3–6 years.
  - After each year's tax return has been filed, retain the appropriate records with a *copy* of that tax return in:
        TAXES (INCOME).

EXPENSES
(EMPLOYMENT & "MISC.")

Expenses Related to Your Employment

- Logs That Contain Information about Each Expense, *Including:*
    Purpose and destination
    Recipients of and business reasons for meals, gifts and
    entertainment
    Travel dates

    Note: *You must have a paid bill or receipt for all expenses over $25.*

- Receipts
    – For all expenses that may be tax deductible because they are
    necessary for your occupation.

- Records of Business-Related Expenses, *Including:*
    Auto mileage
    Books and tuition (required by employer or necessary for
    advancement)
    Tolls
    Union or professional dues
    Work-related moving expenses

"Misc." Expenses Related to Producing Income

- Evidence of "Miscellaneous" Expenses (that may be tax deductible),
    Including:
    Advisory fees for:
        Accountants
        Financial advisers
        Investment managers
        Lawyers
    Home office expenses
    Personal computer costs
    Safe-deposit box fees
    Subscriptions useful to producing income

Helpful Materials

IRS Publications
#463 "Travel, Entertainment & Gift Expenses—What Records To Keep"
#917 "Business Uses of a Car"

See: "List of IRS Publications" in Chapter 9.

EXPENSES
(EMPLOYMENT & "MISC.")

DO NOT FILE HERE

- Other Auto Records
  - Maintenance records, registrations, etc.
    See: **AUTOS, BOATS & RVs**

WHEN TO REMOVE

- Actual Policies
  - Dispose of when there is no possibility of a claim *(see your agent)* *and* the policy has been replaced or the property disposed of.

- Copies of Claims and Insurance Company Check Stubs
  - Dispose of one year after claims are paid.
  - Keep 6 years if papers are evidence of a tax-deductible loss.
  - Evidence of large settlements may be kept with tax records to prove nontaxable income.

- Premium Payment Receipts
  - May be discarded when premium notices properly reflect your past payments.

INSURANCE
AUTOS, BOATS & RVs

FILE HERE

MAKE A SEPARATE MANILA FOLDER FOR EACH VEHICLE.

- List of All Auto Policies
- Actual Policies and Descriptive Brochures
- Check Stubs
  - From claims paid by insurance company
- Copies of Claims You Have Filed
- Copies of Past Accident Records
- Discount Information, *Including:*
  - Student driver course certificates
  - Honor student report cards (for verification of good student discount where available)
  - Antitheft devices
- Information on **How To File Claims**
- Papers and Correspondence
  - Related to accidents and claims
- Premium Payment Receipts or Canceled Checks
- Spare Claims Forms

INSURANCE
AUTOS, BOATS & RVs

DO NOT FILE HERE

- Employee Benefit Descriptions
    - *See:* **EMPLOYMENT**

- Receipts for Medical Bills You Have Paid
    - *See:* **MEDICAL RECORDS**

WHEN TO REMOVE

- Actual Policies
    - Dispose of when they have *totally* expired or lapsed *and* after seeing your agent to be sure whether there is any possibility of a successful claim.
    - Generally, you will not want to let coverage lapse until a new policy is fully effective.

- Copies of Claims and Insurance Company Check Stubs
    - Dispose of one year after claims are paid.
    - Evidence of large settlements may be kept with tax records to prove nontaxable income.

- Premium Payment Receipts
    - May be discarded when premium notices properly reflect your past payments.

Note: In cases where premiums have been deducted from taxable income, retain checks in tax records for 3–6 years.

INSURANCE
HEALTH & DISABILITY

FILE HERE

MAKE A SEPARATE MANILA FOLDER FOR EACH PERSON.

- List of All Health Policies
  See: **Lists in Chapter 6,** "Data Collection Center"

- Actual Policies and Descriptive Brochures

- Check Stubs from Insurance Proceeds

- Copies of Claims You Have Filed

- Information on **How To File Claims** with Your Insurance Company

- Medicare and Medicaid Brochures, Forms and Claims

- Other Correspondence with Your Insurance Company

- Premium Payment Receipts or Canceled Checks

- Spare Claims Forms

DO NOT FILE HERE

- Auto-Related Insurance Information
    See: **INSURANCE (AUTOS, BOATS & RVs)**

- Insurance on Other Real Estate
    See: **REAL ESTATE**

WHEN TO REMOVE

- Actual Policies
    - Dispose of *only* when there is no possibility of a claim *(see your agent)* *and* the policy has been replaced or the property disposed of.

- Copies of Claims and Insurance Company Check Stubs
    - Dispose of one year after claims are paid.
    - Keep 6 years if papers are evidence of a tax-deductible loss.
    - Evidence of large settlements may be kept with tax records to prove nontaxable income.

- Premium Payment Receipts
    - May be disposed of when premium notices properly reflect your past payments.

INSURANCE
HOME & PROPERTY

- List of All:
    Homeowner's policies
    Renter's policies
    Excess liability (umbrella) policies
    See: **Lists in Chapter 6,** "Data Collection Center"

- Actual Policies and Descriptive Brochures

- Appraisals (keep originals in a safe-deposit box)
    Art
    Collectibles
    Furs
    Jewelry

- Check Stubs from Claims Paid by Insurance Company

- Copies of Claims You Have Filed

- Information on **How To File Claims**

- Papers and Correspondence Related to Accidents and Claims

- Photographs of Damaged Property

- Photos of Home and Personal Property (Keep negatives in a safe-deposit box.)

- Premium Payment Receipts or Canceled Checks

- Spare Claims Forms

INSURANCE
HOME & PROPERTY

DO NOT FILE HERE

- Employee Benefit Descriptions
    See: **EMPLOYMENT**

WHEN TO REMOVE

- Death Certificates (after estate is settled)
    – Move to **ARCHIVE: WILLS & TRUSTS**

- Expired or Lapsed Policies
    – Dispose of *only* when there is no cash value *and* when there is no chance of reinstatement (often 5 years). *See your agent.*

- Policy Loan Records
    – Keep 3–6 years with the appropriate year's tax return.
    – If latest record is cumulative, discard older versions.

- Receipts
    – May be discarded when premium notices reflect your payment.

MAKE A SEPARATE MANILA FOLDER FOR EACH POLICY.

- List of All Life and Annuity Policies
    See: **Lists in Chapter 6,** "Data Collection Center"

- All Actual Policies (*Copies* can be kept in a safe-deposit box.)

- Death Certificates
    – Also keep a *copy* in a safe-deposit box and in:
        WILLS & TRUSTS

- Latest Record of Policy Loans

- Latest Record of Policy Proceeds

- Premium Payment Receipts or Canceled Checks

- Your Insurance Needs Worksheets
    – *Review frequently,* especially after any change in employment and any new dependents as a result of birth, marriage, aging parents or other circumstances (e.g., bigger house, new responsibilities, etc.).

INSURANCE
LIFE & ANNUITY

- Employment-Related Investments
  - Such as stock options and 401(k)s

    See: **EMPLOYMENT**

- IRA Account Statements

    See: **RETIREMENT SAVINGS**

- Pension, Profit Sharing, Insurance

    See: "List of Investment Matters" on the next page

WHEN TO REMOVE

- Dividend Check Stubs
  - Discard when all income is properly reflected on your annual 1099 forms.

- Monthly Statements
  - Retain during the year. Each month, examine to be certain that all expected income has been received, that all transaction data matches *confirms* and that all your deposits are correctly recorded. After tax return is prepared, you may discard previous year's monthly statements, but keep *confirms* and 1099s.

- Purchase *Confirms*
  - As evidence of cost, keep 3–6 years after investment is *sold* in
    ARCHIVE: INVESTMENTS

- Sale *Confirms*
  - Dispose of when the transactions are correctly reflected on the monthly statement.

- 1099 Forms and Capital Gains Distribution Records
  - Keep with each year's tax return when it is filed.

INVESTMENTS

FILE HERE

MAKE A SEPARATE MANILA FOLDER FOR EACH INVESTMENT
INSTITUTION: KEEP LIKE STATEMENTS CLIPPED OR STAPLED
TOGETHER IN CHRONOLOGICAL SEQUENCE.

- Check Stubs from Dividends and Interest Received

- Evidence of Liquidation or Worthlessness of Investments

- Investment Account Check-Writing Information

- K-1 Partnership Statements

- List of Investment Matters That You Keep in Other Files, *Including:*
  Retirement, Profit Sharing
  See: **EMPLOYMENT** and **RETIREMENT SAVINGS**

  Investment-Type Insurance Policies
  See: **INSURANCE (LIFE & ANNUITIES)**

- Papers Regarding Loans You Have Made to Others

- Partnership Agreements and Prospectuses

- Regular Statements, *Including:*
  Bank CDs, etc.
  Brokerage accounts
  Limited partnerships
  Mutual funds

- 1099 Forms, *Including:*
  Records of Capital Gains Distributions and Reinvested Dividends

- Transaction Receipts (Confirms)

INVESTMENTS

DO NOT FILE HERE

- Medical Insurance-Related Papers, Records, Claims and Receipts for Premiums

    See: **INSURANCE (HEALTH & DISABILITY)**

WHEN TO REMOVE

If Expenses Result in a Tax Deduction
   – Keep with that year's tax return for 3–6 years.

If Expenses DO NOT Result in a Tax Deduction
   – Discard receipts when they are not needed to support claims *and* when you have recorded any pertinent information in each person's medical history.

Note: *For making future decisions regarding selection of healthcare coverage, you may find it helpful to keep in the* **Medical Records** *file a list of individual healthcare claims experiences.*

MEDICAL RECORDS

MAKE A SEPARATE MANILA FOLDER FOR EACH FAMILY MEMBER.

- Personal Medical Records of Family Members, *Including:*

  Allergies, etc.   Childhood diseases
  Blood type   Lab test results
  Boosters   Shots

- Appointment Cards

- Correspondence Concerning Health Matters

- List of Medical Professionals Visited During the Year (This should become a cumulative list.)

  Dentists
  Family doctors
  Hospitals
  Therapists, etc.

- Receipts of Paid Healthcare Bills, *Including:*

  Dentist   Medical appliances, etc.
  Doctor   Prescription medicine
  Hospital   Therapist

  – It may be useful to *make copies before you send the original* medical bills to your insurance company so that you will be able to update your "Medical Histories."

- Record of Travel Expenses Related to Healthcare

- Treatment Plans and Long-Term Medication Needs

- Written General Medical History

Note: *This can be very helpful for future reference. Update yearly with general health summary, citing any illnesses, surgeries and other medical information.*

MEDICAL RECORDS

DO NOT FILE HERE

- Children's Artwork
- Mementos
- Recipes
- Other Family Photos

Note: Make separate labeled boxes or files to store these kinds of valuable items. (See: Chapter 10, "Saving Other 'Stuff.'")

WHEN TO REMOVE

- Outdated Passports May Be Destroyed and Disposed Of.
- Retain Military Papers for Possible Veterans Benefits.

PERSONAL

FILE HERE

MAKE A SEPARATE MANILA FOLDER FOR EACH FAMILY MEMBER, INCLUDING PARENTS IF YOU ARE RESPONSIBLE FOR THEIR RECORDS.

MAKE A SEPARATE MANILA FOLDER FOR FAMILY PETS.

Copies of the following original documents should be kept in this file for reference. Originals should be stored in your safe-deposit box or fireproof safe to protect them from fire or theft.

- Adoption of Naturalization Papers
- Certificates, *Including:*
     Birth, death
     Marriage, divorce, separation
     Religious ceremonies
- Court Orders on Personal Matters Such as Child Custody and Support
- Diplomas
- Fingerprints of Each Family Member
- Military Discharge Papers
- Passports

You May Also Want To Keep in This File
- Awards and Publicity
- Current Photo of Each Family Member
- Documents Relating to Family Pets
- Miscellaneous Personal Papers
- Organization Membership Papers

PERSONAL

DO NOT FILE HERE

- Homeowner's Insurance on Residence
    See: **INSURANCE (HOME & PROPERTY)**

- Primary Residence Information
    See: **RESIDENCE**

- Real Estate Partnership Information
    See: **INVESTMENTS**

WHEN TO REMOVE

- Real Estate Records (other than your residence)
    - They are best kept 3–6 years after a property has been disposed of *and* all related taxes (especially capital gains) have been paid.
    - For properties you have disposed of by sale or gift, records may be moved to:
        ARCHIVE: REAL ESTATE
    (after each year's tax return is filed.)
    - In cases of *tax swaps*, keep records indefinitely in:
        ARCHIVE: REAL ESTATE

REAL ESTATE

FILE HERE

MAKE A SEPARATE MANILA FOLDER FOR EACH PROPERTY.

- *Copies* of Deeds, Titles and Title Insurance (*Originals* should be kept in a safe-deposit box.)

- Cumulative List of Properties Bought and Sold, *Including:*
    Purchase costs
    Sales proceeds for each property
        See: **Lists in Chapter 6,** "Data Collection Center"

- For Inherited Property
    Copies of estate tax returns
    Other evidence of your *cost basis* for tax purposes

- Insurance Information on Properties Owned

- Mortgage Information and Receipts

- Other Closing Papers, *Including:*
    Receipts
    Canceled checks

- Real Estate Tax Notices

- Receipts for All Improvements, *Including:*
    Specific property involved
    Date expense was incurred
    Nature and cost of improvement

If You Rent Property to Others

- *Copies* of Leases or Rental Agreements (*originals* should be kept in a safe-deposit box.)

- Rental Income and Expense Records, *Including:*
    Number of days rented
    Amount of personal use
    Records of security deposits
    Advertisements, evidence of attempts to rent
    Rental agent information
    All receipts and records related to this "business"

REAL ESTATE

DO NOT FILE HERE

- Home Insurance Information
  See: **INSURANCE (HOME & PROPERTY)**

- Information about Other Real Estate Owned
  See: **REAL ESTATE**

WHEN TO REMOVE

- Keep Residential Records Indefinitely in
  ARCHIVE: RESIDENCE

RESIDENCE

If You Own Your Residence
- Annual Statements from Mortgagee (Lender), *Including:*
  – Principal, interest, escrow information and real estate taxes

- *Copies* of Purchase-Related Documents (Originals should be kept in a safe-deposit box or fireproof box.), *Including:*

Appraisal	Mortgage
Closing papers	Sales contract
Deed	Survey

- Legal Proceedings Regarding Property
  – Such as purchase or sale of easement, condemnation of property, etc.

- Mortgage and Tax Receipts or Canceled Checks

- Property Owners or Neighborhood Association Information

- Real Estate Tax and Assessment Papers

- Receipts for Improvements
  – Keep even after sale of residence because the *cost basis* of one residence affects the *basis* of subsequent ones.

  See: **Lists in Chapter 6,** "Data Collection Center"

- Records of Uninsured Casualty Losses Related to Home

If Your Residence Was Inherited
- Keep Estate or Inheritance Tax Return Showing Property Value

If You Rent Your Residence
- *Copy* of Your Lease
- Correspondence and Agreements Concerning Residence
- Rent Receipts or Canceled Checks

If You Use Your Residence for a Business

See: **SELF-EMPLOYED**

Helpful Materials

IRS Publications
523 "Tax Information on Selling Your Home"
2119 "Sale or Exchange of Principal Residence"
587 "Business Uses of Your Home"

RESIDENCE

DO NOT FILE HERE

- Annuities
    - *See:* **INSURANCE (LIFE & ANNUITIES)**

- Other Investments
    - *See:* **INVESTMENTS**

- Records for Employer-Sponsored Pension or Retirement Programs *while You Are Actively Working*
    - *See:* **EMPLOYMENT**

- Social Security Records
    - *See:* **SOCIAL SECURITY**

WHEN TO REMOVE

- Deposit Receipts
    - May be discarded when they have been correctly recorded on your account statements.

- Statements
    - Save for 3–6 years in
        - **ARCHIVE: RETIREMENT SAVINGS**

- Nondeductible IRAs
    - Keep records indefinitely.

MAKE A SEPARATE MANILA FOLDER FOR EACH INSTITUTION.

- Copies of Documents Establishing Your Plans

- Documents Concerning IRA Rollovers and Transfers

- Documents Needed To Determine Your Income Tax Liability When You Start Making Withdrawals at Retirement
  - If you make deductible *and* nondeductible IRA contributions, records of the latter should be kept for life! Keep these two kinds of IRAs in separate accounts.

- Forms, *Including:*
  5498
  RRBW-2P
  1099-R or other evidence of pension income
  W-2P

- Information Concerning Loans from Tax-Deferred Accounts

- IRA and Keogh Records

- Records of Withdrawals from IRAs and Keoghs

- Statements from Custodians of IRA or other Tax-Deferred Retirement Accounts Showing:
  Accumulated assets
  Disbursements
  Investments
  Receipts

- 1099 Forms for IRA Accounts

- Your Personal Retirement Plan

When You Are Retired

- Records of All Distributions from Plans

- Records of All Pension Income Received

- Statements Breaking Down Pension Income into Taxable and Nontaxable Components

RETIREMENT SAVINGS

DO NOT FILE HERE

- Charitable Solicitations from Schools
  - *See:* **CHARITIES**

- Diplomas and Certificates
  - *See:* **PERSONAL**

- Kids' "Stuff," Artwork, Etc.
  - *See:* **Chapter 9,** "Saving Other 'Stuff' "

- School Accident Insurance Policies
  - *See:* **INSURANCE (HEALTH & DISABILITY)**

- Tuition Loan Information
  - *See:* **CREDIT**

WHEN TO REMOVE

- If School Courses Are Related to Employment (hence potentially tax deductible), Put Information with That Year's Tax Return in
  - **TAXES (INCOME)**

- W10 and W2 Forms
  - – Put information with that year's tax return in
    - **TAXES (INCOME)**

- Brochures, Course Descriptions You Want To Save

- Correspondence with:
  Schools
  Day care
  Camps, etc.

- Financial Aid Forms, Instructions and Information

- Forms
  W10 for childcare expenses
  W2 for childcare workers you employ in your home

- Receipts and Records of Paid Bills for All Family Members, *Including:*
  Tuition
  Books
  Fees, etc.

- Receipts for Childcare Wages Paid

- School and College Applications

- Transcripts of Grades

SCHOOLS & CHILDCARE

DO NOT FILE HERE

- Keogh Records Related to Self-Employment
      See: **RETIREMENT SAVINGS**

- Records of Expenses Incurred Due to Your Employment by Someone Else
      See: **EXPENSES (EMPLOYMENT & "MISC.")**

WHEN TO REMOVE

At Your Earliest Opportunity
   – Move items to an actual business filing system set up specifically for your self-employment activity.

- Tax-Related Records
   – Should be kept 3–6 years.
   – After each year's tax return has been filed, save relevant self-employment records with your copy of that tax return in
         TAXES (INCOME)

MAKE A SEPARATE SET OF FILES AND ACCOUNTING RECORDS FOR EVEN A SMALL BUSINESS (A SEPARATE SET FOR *EACH* VENTURE).

Note: This "Self-Employed" file may provide a place to keep track of information related to a very small sideline business or start-up records until you initiate a business file system.

- Bank and Credit Card Records Related to the Business
  – If business charges are on your personal credit records, place *copies* here and indicate the business aspects on these copies.

- Business Insurance Records

- Employee, Independent Contractor and Domestic Employee Records
  – E.g., pay, tax and benefits information.

- Expense Records Such as Receipts for

Entertainment	Subscriptions
Equipment	Supplies
Inventory	Travel
Professional Services	Other

- Latest-Year Tax Records Relating to the Business Activity

- Record of Interest Paid on Business-Related Debt

- Record of Personal Use of Business Assets

- Records of Credit Extended, *Including:*
    Efforts to collect
    Interest charged
    Payments received

- Sales and Income Records, *Including:*
    Commissions received
    Contracts
    Sales receipts

HELPFUL MATERIALS

IRS Publications
#334 "Small Business Guide"
#587 "Business Uses of Your Home"

SELF-EMPLOYED

DO NOT FILE HERE

- Information Related to Private Pension Plans
    See: **EMPLOYMENT**

- IRA and Keogh Records
    See: **RETIREMENT SAVINGS**

- Medicare and Medicaid Information
    See: **INSURANCE (HEALTH & DISABILITY)**

WHEN TO REMOVE

- Earlier Earnings History Statements
    – Discard as you receive current records of your payments into the Social Security system.

- Historical Data
    – Move to
        ARCHIVE: SOCIAL SECURITY

FILE HERE

- All Correspondence with the Social Security Administration

- List of Social Security Numbers
  - Of all family members, *including:*
      Children
      Deceased members
      Parents
      Separated, widowed, divorced members
      Other members for whom you may be caregiver

- Personal Earnings History for Each Member
  - Send for current status of Social Security earnings for each member every few years.

- Records of Social Security Income received

Helpful Material

For personal earnings history, request
IRS Publication #SSA-7004PC-OP1

SOCIAL SECURITY

DO NOT FILE HERE

- Business Records
  - *See:* **SELF-EMPLOYED** and **EXPENSES**

- Current Year Tax-Related Information
  - 1099 forms
    - *See:* **INVESTMENTS** and **BANK ACCOUNTS**

  - Healthcare Receipts
    - *See:* **MEDICAL RECORDS**

  - Inheritance and Trust Income
    - *See:* **WILLS & TRUSTS**

  - Records of Charitable Donations
    - *See:* **CHARITIES**

  - W-2 Forms
    - *See:* **EMPLOYMENT, SELF-EMPLOYED** and **SCHOOLS**

- Real Estate Tax Information
  - *See:* **RESIDENCE** and **REAL ESTATE**

- Tax Returns for Trusts or Business Entities
  - *See:* **WILLS & TRUSTS** and **SELF-EMPLOYED**

WHEN TO REMOVE

After the Latest Year's Tax Return Has Been Completed
- Keep *your copy* in this file with its supporting documents.

- Place *your previous year's copy* in:
  ARCHIVE: TAXES (INCOME)

Note: *The IRS has 3 years to raise routine questions about your tax return; 6 years if it thinks you "substantially" underreported income. In cases of fraud, there is no time limitation. (Tax advisers recommend keeping records 6 years.)*

TAXES (INCOME)

- Canceled Checks for Taxes Paid

- *Copies* of Estimated Tax Returns

- *Copies* of Requests for Extensions

- Correspondence with Tax Authorities
  – Along with supporting documents

- Federal and State Income Tax Returns
  – Only for the most recent year
  – Attach supporting documents

- Records, *Including:*
         Alimony payments or receipts
         Gambling income and losses
         Prizes and awards

WHEN YOU BEGIN TO PREPARE YOUR TAX RETURN

Move tax-related papers from other files to this one. Thenceforth, retain these documents with your copy of the appropriate year's tax return.
See: **Chapter 9,** "The IRS and Your Files!"

TAXES (INCOME)

DO NOT FILE HERE

- Handbooks, Warranties and Receipts
  - Related to autos, boats and recreational vehicles
    - *See:* **AUTOS, BOATS & RVs**

- Receipts and Warranties for Improvements Made to
  - Primary Residence
    - *See:* **RESIDENCE**
  - Other Real Estate Owned
    - *See:* **REAL ESTATE**

WHEN TO REMOVE

- Receipts
  - Ask yourself if the receipt may be needed to:
    - Establish value of the purchase for:
      - Insurance claims
      - Resale, etc.
    - Facilitate a return to the seller
    - Support tax deductions
  - Use judgment in discarding.

- User Handbooks and Instructions
  - Discard when items are no longer owned.

- Warranties
  - Discard when they are *clearly expired.*

WARRANTIES & RECEIPTS

FILE HERE

IF YOU HAVE A SUBSTANTIAL NUMBER OF RECEIPTS & WARRANTIES, MAKE A MANILA FOLDER FOR EACH OF THE FOLLOWING FIVE CATEGORIES:

- Any Purchase Receipts You Feel You May Need in the Future
  - To evidence an item's value
  - For merchandise returns

- Maintenance Contracts *Including:*
     Air conditioner, etc.
     Appliances
     Furnace
     Telephone

- Maintenance Records for Items Mentioned Above

- Owner's Manuals and Handbooks for Appliances, Etc.

- Warranties Pertaining to:
     Appliances
     Clothing
     Computers
     Electronic equipment, etc.
     Equipment
     Furniture

  - Also include *receipts* showing purchases of these items.
  - Staple receipts to warranties.

WARRANTIES & RECEIPTS

DO NOT FILE HERE

- *Originals* of Wills or Trusts if You Have a Safer Place
- Probate of an Estate
  - Ideally, create a separate set of files to track the extensive proceedings, documentation and tax returns related to probate.

WHEN TO REMOVE

- Estate or Trust Tax Returns *Older* than the Immediately Preceding Year
  - Move to
    ### ARCHIVE: WILLS & TRUSTS
- Information That May Have Tax Implications
  - Should be kept at least 6 years after the liquidation or termination of a trust or probate of an estate.
- When a Trust Has Been Terminated or Legally Rendered Obsolete
  - Move copy to
    ### ARCHIVE: WILLS & TRUSTS
  - Indicate on copy that it is obsolete.
- When Your Will Has Been Rendered Obsolete (by an entirely new version)
  - You may dispose of the *copies* of the old one.
  - Old *original* should also be destroyed.

WILLS & TRUSTS

FILE HERE

Note: Originals of wills and trust documents should be kept in a fireproof box in your home or other location which you record in Chapter 6, "Data Collection Center." (DO NOT keep original will in a safe-deposit box, which could be sealed upon a person's death!) A copy may be filed with the Registrar of Wills in your jurisdiction or kept by your attorney or your personal representative. (See: Chapter 8, "The Safety Factor and Your Files!")

- *Copies* of Trust Documents, *Including:*
  Trusts established *for your benefit* by others
  Trusts for which you are the *trustee*
  Trusts *you* have established

- *Copies* of Wills

- Correspondence Related to Wills and Trusts

- Documentation of Gifts
  – Gifts in excess of the annual exclusion amount
  – Significant nontaxable gifts

- Documents Concerning Income and Assets of Trusts

- K-1 Schedule for Trusts

- Trust Tax Return from Latest Year

WILLS & TRUSTS

The Quick-Find Index is one of the best-loved features of the HOMEFILE® system. The index lists in alphabetical order more than 200 different kinds of personal papers and documents that typically need to be kept track of. For each of these items, the index identifies the appropriate file category!

Category Choices

Sometimes the Quick-Find Index indicates more than one potential file location for a document. For example, casualty loss records could be filed either under "Insurance (Home & Property)" or under "Insurance (Auto)." The choice, of course, depends on what kind of casualty is involved... whether the documents relate to an automotive casualty loss or another kind of property loss.

Whenever more than one file is listed in the index for a document, it will be obvious how you should make the selection. For example, a choice between "Residence" and "Real Estate" frequently occurs. In these cases, you will choose "Residence" if your documents relate to your principal home and "Real Estate" if they involve some other real property such as a vacation home or rental unit that you own.

Customizing
Your Index

HOMEFILE® users can customize the index for their own personal use. The "Information Age" has brought endless kinds of information to our fingertips. We all have many kinds of important papers for everything from AA to the Zoo's Friends. Because everyone's filing needs are different, it is obviously impossible to anticipate and include every possibility in the index. However, we wanted to make your HOMEFILE® system thoroughly adaptable to your individual needs, so we created an index in which you can enter, alphabetically, your unique personal filing items that are not listed in the standard index. In the column labeled "Personal Supplemental Index," you simply write the name of the item that you wish to include in your file under the correct alphabetical section, then under it write what file you placed it in.

For example, you may have a personal commitment to and involvement in the Boy Scouts, which does not appear in the standard index. You may write it on the lines next to the "B" section of the index and indicate in which file you placed the relevant papers, such as the "Personal" file or "Charities."

Perhaps you have formed a garden club with some friends. The principal activity is that you pool your orders for shrubbery to get wholesale prices. You have some order slips that you could file under "Receipts." You have some club meeting minutes that might go under "Personal." You use the shrubs to landscape both your year-round home and your house at the beach, so maybe either "Residence" or "Real Estate" is the appropriate place to file receipts for tax records.

With the Personal Supplemental Index, all you have to do is decide where you want to keep these garden club records and write it in the left-hand column. That way, when you need the minutes or the receipts, just look up "Garden Club," and you'll see where you decided to file them. You can even make several different entries, such as:

Garden Club (receipts)… RESIDENCE
Garden Club (minutes)… PERSONAL

PERSONAL SUPPLEMENTAL INDEX	DOCUMENT	FILE CATEGORY

— F —

Fees, Advisory	Expenses (Employment & "Misc.")
Financial Aid Forms	Schools & Childcare
Financial Statements	
Personal	Credit
Forms	
401 (k)	Employment
403 (b)	Employment
1099	
(as indep. contractor)	Employment
(by issuer)	Bank Accounts
	Investments
W-2, W-10	*See* W (this Index)
Furnace	
Maintenance Contract	Warranties & Receipts

— G , H —

Gambling Records	Taxes (Income)
Gifts	Wills & Trusts
Health Insurance	Insurance: Health & Disability
Home Office	Expenses (Employment & "Misc.")
Expense Records	Self-Employed
House Lease, Copy	Residence
	Real Estate

PERSONAL SUPPLEMENTAL INDEX entries:

FILE: _____

FILE: _____

Garden Club (MINUTES)
PERSONAL
FILE: _____

Garden Club (receipts)
RESIDENCE
FILE: _____

However, be sure to read through Chapter 10, "Saving Other 'Stuff,'" before attempting to add too much to your current files. There may be a better way for you to save other "stuff."

The Quick-Find Index

FILE: _____

FILE: _____

FILE: _____

FILE: _____

FILE: _____

FILE: _____

FILE: _____

FILE: _____

FILE: _____

FILE: _____

——— A ———

Accident
    Vehicle ....Insurance (Autos, Boats & RVs)
    Other ....Insurance (Health & Disability)
                  Insurance (Home & Property)
Accountant's Fees ....Expenses (Employment & "Misc.")
Adoption Papers ....Personal
AKC Papers ....Personal (Pet Folder)
Alimony
    Payments or Receipts ....Taxes (Income)
Allergy ....Medical Records
Annuity ....Insurance (Life & Annuities)
Apartment Lease ....Residence
Appliance
    Maintenance Contracts ....Warranties & Receipts
Appointments
    Medical, Dental ....Medical Records
Appraisals ....Charities
                  Insurance (Home & Property)
Auto Insurance ....Insurance (Autos, Boats & RVs)
Auto Loan Records ....Credit
Awards, Personal ....Personal

——— B ———

Bank Records
    Personal ....Bank Accounts
    Business ....Self-Employed
Baptismal Certificate ....Personal
Benefits Description ....Employment
Birth Certificate ....Personal
Blood Type ....Medical Records
Boat Insurance ....Insurance (Autos, Boats & RVs)
Boat Records ....Autos, Boats & RVs
Book Expenses ....Schools & Childcare
Brochures
    Schools, Camps ....Schools & Childcare
Broker Statements ....Investments
                  Retirement Savings

——— C ———

Camp Records ....Schools & Childcare
Canceled Checks
    Tax-Related ....Charities
                  Expenses (Employment & "Misc.")
                  Insurance (Health & Disability)
                  Medical Records
                  Real Estate
                  Residence
                  Self-Employed
                  Taxes (Income)
Casualty Loss ....Insurance (Autos, Boats & RVs)
                  Insurance (Home & Property)
Catalogs, School ....Schools & Childcare
CD
    Tax-Deferred ....Retirement Savings
    Taxable ....Investments

FILE: _____

FILE: _____

FILE: _____

FILE: _____

FILE: _____

FILE: _____

FILE: _____

FILE: _____

FILE: _____

FILE: _____

Document	File Category
Cemetery Deeds	Wills & Trusts
Charities	Charities
Checking Account Statements	Bank Accounts
Child Support, Custody	Personal
Church Donations	Charities
Claims, Insurance	
Medical	Insurance (Health & Disability)
Property	Insurance (Autos, Boats & RVs)
	Insurance (Home & Property)
Closing Papers	Real Estate
	Residence
Code Numbers	
Bank	Bank Accounts
Credit Cards	Credit
Collection Records	Investments
	Real Estate
	Self-Employed
College Applications	Schools & Childcare
Confirmations	
Stocks and Bonds, Etc.	Investments
	Retirement Savings
Contracts	
Business	Self-Employed
Home Repairs	Residence
Repair Other Property	Real Estate
Contract, Sale or Purchase	
Auto	Autos, Boats & RVs
Primary Home	Residence
Real Estate	Real Estate
Credit Card	
Business	Expenses (Employment & "Misc.")
	Self-Employed
Personal	Credit
Credit Union Papers	Bank Accounts

— D —

Document	File Category
Day Care	Schools & Childcare
Death Certificate	Insurance (Life & Annuities)
	Personal
	Safe-Deposit Boxes
	Wills & Trusts
Deed	
Cemetery	Wills & Trusts
Real Estate (Copies)	Real Estate
	Residence
Deferred Compensation	Employment
Deposit Records	
Bank and Credit Union	Bank Accounts
Insurance	Insurance (Life & Annuities)
IRA/Keogh	Retirement Savings
Diplomas	Personal
Disability	
Income	Insurance (Health & Disability)
Insurance	Insurance (Health & Disability)
Dividend Records	
Insurance	Insurance (Life & Annuities)
Stock	Investments
	Retirement Savings
Divorce Papers	Personal

PERSONAL SUPPLEMENTAL INDEX	DOCUMENT	FILE CATEGORY

_____

_____

FILE: _____

_____

_____

FILE: _____

_____

_____

FILE: _____

_____

_____

FILE: _____

_____

_____

FILE: _____

_____

_____

FILE: _____

_____

_____

FILE: _____

_____

_____

FILE: _____

_____

_____

FILE: _____

_____

_____

FILE: _____

Doctor Appointments .... Medical Records
Dues, Records of .... Expenses (Employment & "Misc.")

—— E ——

Earnings History .... Social Security
Easement .... Real Estate
                                             Residence
Employee
      Benefits .... Employment
      Handbook .... Employment
Employer Information .... Employment
Equipment
      Maintenance Contracts .... Warranties & Receipts
Escrow .... Real Estate
                                             Residence
Expenses, Business .... Expenses (Employment & "Misc.")
                                             Self-Employed

—— F ——

Fees, Advisory .... Expenses (Employment & "Misc.")
Financial Aid Forms .... Schools & Childcare
Financial Statements
      Personal .... Credit
Forms
      401(k) .... Employment
      403 (b) .... Employment
      1099
          (As indep. contractor) .... Employment
          (By issuer) .... Bank Accounts
                                           Investments
      W-2, W-10 .... _See_ W (this Index)
Furnace
      Maintenance Contract .... Warranties & Receipts

—— G , H ——

Gambling Records .... Taxes (Income)
Gifts .... Wills & Trusts
Health Insurance .... Insurance (Health & Disability)
Home Office
      Expense Records .... Expenses (Employment & "Misc.")
                                             Self-Employed
House Lease, Copy .... Real Estate
                                             Residence

—— I ——

Improvements, Home .... Residence
Inheritance
      General .... Wills & Trusts
      Of Residence .... Residence
Inspection
      Autos, Boats, Etc. .... Autos, Boats & RVs

FILE: _____	
FILE: _____	
FILE: _____	
FILE: _____	
FILE: _____	
FILE: _____	
FILE: _____	
FILE: _____	
FILE: _____	
FILE: _____	

Insurance

> Business and Professional .... Expenses (Employment & "Misc.")
> Self-Employed
>> Claims .... *See* Claims (This Index)
>> Needs Worksheets .... Insurance (Life & Annuities)
>> Policies .... Insurance (Autos, Boats & RVs)
>> Insurance (Health & Disability)
>> Insurance (Home & Property)
>> Insurance (Life & Annuities)

Interest (Paid)

> Business Loans .... Self-Employed
> Expenses (Employment & "Misc.")
>> Personal .... Credit
>> Investment
>> Real Estate
>> Residence

Interest (Received) .... Bank Accounts
> Investments
> Retirement Savings

IRA .... Retirement Savings

—— K , L ——

K-1

> Partnerships .... Investments
> Trusts .... Wills & Trusts

Keys' Location .... *See* Chapter 6

Laboratory Tests

> Medical .... Medical Records

Lease Agreements

> As Landlord .... Real Estate
> As Tenant .... Residence

Legal Proceedings .... Insurance (Autos, Boats & RVs)
(according to type of issue)   Insurance (Health & Disability)
> Insurance (Home & Property)
> Insurance (Life & Annuities)
> Personal
> Real Estate
> Residence

License

> Autos, Boats .... Autos, Boats & RVs
> Guns, Fishing, Etc. .... Personal

Life Insurance .... Insurance (Life & Annuities)

Limited Partnership .... Investments
> Retirement Savings

Loans

> Applications & Records .... Credit
> From Insurance Policy .... Insurance (Life & Annuities)
> Made to Others .... Investments
> From Retirement Plans .... Employment
> Retirement Savings
>> Tuition .... Credit

Locks .... *See* Chapter 6

Logs, Business .... Expenses (Employment & "Misc.")
> Self-Employed

—— M ——

Maintenance Records
    Autos, Boats, Etc. .... Autos, Boats & RVs
    Nonautomotive .... Warranties & Receipts
Manuals
    Autos, Boats, Etc. .... Autos, Boats & RVs
    Other .... Warranties & Receipts
Marriage Certificate .... Personal
Medical
    History .... Medical Records
    Insurance .... Insurance (Health & Disability)
    Medicaid, Medicare .... Insurance (Health & Disability)
    Medication Needs, Records .... Medical Records
    Receipts .... Medical Records
Membership Papers .... Personal
Mileage Records, Auto .... Charities
                                      Expenses (Employment & "Misc.")
                                      Medical Records
                                      Self-Employed
Military
    Records, Discharge Papers .... Personal
Mortgage
    Loans Made to Others .... Investments
    On Primary Home .... Residence
    On Other Property .... Real Estate
Moving Expense Records .... Expenses (Employment & "Misc.")
Mutual Fund .... Investments
                                      Retirement Savings

—— N , O ——

Naturalization Papers .... Personal
Neighborhood Association .... Residence
Organization Papers .... Personal
Owner's Handbooks
    Appliances, Etc. .... Warranties & Receipts
    Autos, Boats, Etc. .... Autos, Boats & RVs

—— P ——

Partnership Statements
    K-1 .... Investments
                                        Retirement Savings
Passports .... Personal
Paycheck Stubs .... Employment
Pension Income Received .... Retirement Savings
                                      Social Security
Pets .... Personal (Pet Folder)
Photos
    Of Property .... Insurance (Home & Property)
    Of Family Members .... Personal
Pledges .... Charities
Policy
    Insurance .... *See* Insurance (This Index)
    Loans .... Insurance (Life & Annuities)
Prizes Received .... Personal
                                        Taxes (Income)

FILE: _____

FILE: _____

FILE: _____

FILE: _____

FILE: _____

FILE: _____

FILE: _____

FILE: _____

FILE: _____

FILE: _____

FILE: _____	
FILE: _____	
FILE: _____	
FILE: _____	
FILE: _____	
FILE: _____	
FILE: _____	
FILE: _____	
FILE: _____	
FILE: _____	

—— **R** ——

Real Estate
   Assessment ....Real Estate
                               Residence
Real Estate Taxes ....Real Estate
                               Residence
Recall
   Autos, Etc. ....Autos, Boats & RVs
Receipts
   Autos, Boats, Etc. ....Autos, Boats & RVs
   Business-Related ....Expenses (Employment & "Misc.")
                               Self-Employed
   Charitable..Charities
   General ....Warranties & Receipts
   Medical Bills Paid ....Medical Records
   Real Estate Improvement ....Real Estate
                               Residence
Registration
   Autos, Boats, Etc. ....Autos, Boats & RVs
Rent
   Income Received ....Real Estate
   Paid ....Residence
Resumes ....Employment
Retirement
   IRA, Keogh ....Retirement Savings
   Plan (Employer-sponsored) ....Employment

—— **S** ——

Safe-Deposit Boxes
   Contents .... *See* Chapter 6
   Record of Fees ....Expenses (Employment & "Misc.")
Sales Records, Business ....Self-Employed
Savings Accounts
   Statements & Books ....Bank Accounts
School
   Accident Insurance ....Insurance (Health & Disability)
   Donations ....Charities
   Records, Brochures ....Schools & Childcare
Services, Armed
   Military Records ....Personal
Social Security
   Income Received ....Social Security
   Numbers, Cards ....Social Security
Stock Options...Employment
Student Driver Records..........................Insurance (Autos, Boats & RVs)
Subscription Receipts
   Business...Expenses (Employment & "Misc.")
                               Self-Employed
   Nonbusiness ....Warranties & Receipts

—— T ——

Tax Papers, Real Estate
 Primary Residence ....Residence
 Other Property ....Real Estate
Tax Returns, Income
 (Personal) ....Taxes (Income)
 (Estate or Trust) ....Wills & Trusts
Telephone Credit Cards ....Credit
Tickets
 Traffic & Parking ....Autos, Boats & RVs
Title
 Autos, Boats, Etc. ....Autos, Boats & RVs
 Documents (Real Estate) ....Real Estate
 Residence
 Insurance (Home) ....Residence
 Insurance (Other) ....Real Estate
Transaction
 Receipts (Brokers) ....Investments
 Retirement Savings
Transcripts
 Of Grades ....Schools & Childcare
Travel Costs
 (Depending on purposes) ....Charities
 Expenses (Employment & "Misc.")
 Medical Records
 Self-Employed
Trust
 Documents (Copies) ....Wills & Trusts
Tuition
 Loans ....Credit
 Records (Business-related) ....Expenses (Employment & "Misc.")
 Self-Employed
 (Personal) ....Schools & Childcare

—— U , V , W ——

Unemployment Records ....Employment
Vaccination ....Medical Records
Veterinarian ....Personal (Pet Folder)
W-10 Forms
 Childcare ....Schools & Childcare
W-2 Forms
 Domestic Employees ....Self Employed
 Personal ....Employment
 Your Childcare Worker's ....Schools & Childcare
Warranties
 Autos, Boats, Etc. ....Autos, Boats & RVs
 Other ....Warranties & Receipts
Wills
 Copies ....Wills & Trusts
 Originals...Fireproof Safe
Withdrawal Records
 Banks ....Bank Accounts
 Insurance ....Insurance (Life & Annuity)
 IRA/Keogh ....Retirement Savings

FILE: ——————————

FILE: ——————————

FILE: ——————————

FILE: ——————————

FILE: ——————————

FILE: ——————————

FILE: ——————————

FILE: ——————————

FILE: ——————————

The Archives: Near Yet Far

Files Too Crowded?

One of the most virulent enemies of efficient home filing is *overcrowding*. You know, an insurance file that still has the policies from your first five automobiles! A medical file where you stashed the hospital bills from the birth of your daughter, who now lives in Connecticut with her husband and three children!

When files become seriously overcrowded, they cause us stress. So we tend to avoid using them. Sometimes we are able to grit our teeth and jam one more paper into an overloaded file . . . but we sure regret it when we need to retrieve something!

Two Solutions

The HOMEFILE® system tackles the overcrowding problem in two ways. First, each active category description has a "When To Remove" section that gives guidelines for disposing of documents that you no longer need. This is a big help because nobody wants to throw away something they may need later.

Second, the HOMEFILE® system provides archive files for those categories in which you actually *do* want to save documents indefinitely. We think you will find that setting aside a separate space for storing long-term records will help enormously by freeing up your active files. They will become much more efficient and pleasant to use when the contents are limited to current materials.

The federal government houses our nation's valuable documents in nearly a million cubic feet within marble and granite walls. Hopefully, your archive needs will be much more modest! For example, if there is enough room in the cabinet where you keep your active files, it should work out fine to keep your archives there as well. You can color code the name tabs so that you can distinguish the archives from the active sections at a glance.

However, if it is more convenient to keep your long-term records somewhere else, most office supply stores carry sturdy cardboard filing boxes that will probably meet your requirements for archive storage. Choose a dry place, free from extremes of temperature and as fireproof as possible (See: Chapter 8, "The Safety Factor and Your Files!"). Try to avoid damp basement areas or places that could flood.

Tax preparation time is ideally suited for pruning your files because you will be examining so many of your records anyway. Take the opportunity to pull nonessential papers and get your files in fighting trim for the next 12 months.

Making Archive Notes

There are ten categories for which it is usually appropriate to establish archive files. We suggest that in each archive file you make a list of the contents as you add papers to it. Sometimes it is easier to look for something on your list than to rummage through a pile of papers looking for something that may not even be there!

You may also want to write down the location of related things that you have saved someplace other than the files. For example, you might write on your "Bank Accounts

Archive" page that your old checkbook registers are stored in the upstairs hall closet because they were just too bulky to keep in this file.

Archive Categories

BANK ACCOUNTS
CREDIT
EMPLOYMENT
INVESTMENTS
REAL ESTATE
RESIDENCE
RETIREMENT SAVINGS
SOCIAL SECURITY
TAXES (INCOME)
WILLS & TRUSTS

Sample Archive Page

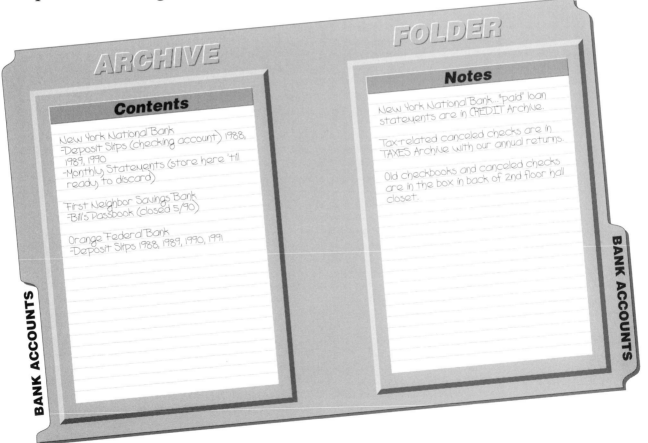

ARCHIVE

Contents

FOLDER

Notes

BANK ACCOUNTS

ARCHIVE

Contents

FOLDER

Notes

CREDIT

ARCHIVE

Contents

FOLDER

Notes

EMPLOYMENT

ARCHIVE

Contents

INVESTMENTS

FOLDER

Notes

INVESTMENTS

ARCHIVE

Contents

FOLDER

Notes

REAL ESTATE

ARCHIVE

Contents

FOLDER

Notes

ARCHIVE

Contents

FOLDER

Notes

ARCHIVE

Contents

FOLDER

Notes

ARCHIVE

Contents

FOLDER

Notes

TAXES (INCOME)

ARCHIVE

Contents

FOLDER

Notes

WILLS & TRUSTS

Data Collection Center

6

Creating Your Personal
Information System

"Floating" Information

As we said earlier, we live in the "Information Age." Sometimes *data* seems to be the fuel that drives our everyday activities—if we run out of it, everything grinds to a halt!

Whenever we call an insurance agent, go to the Motor Vehicle Administration, deal with an automated teller machine, apply for a credit card or open an investment account, we need numbers: account numbers, phone numbers, addresses, Social Security numbers, birth dates, secret code numbers or policy numbers.

So many names, numbers and instructions are necessary for our daily lives to function smoothly. A lot of this information is what we call the "floating" variety; it floats all around our life, some on plastic cards, some buried in documents, some in phone books and some just in our memory! Wouldn't it be great to have it all in one handy place?

Personal Information Lists

We have prepared *personal information lists* to provide a convenient place to gather these kinds of floating data all into one simple location from the dozens of places where they may all be presently lodged. This strategy will make your personal information easily accessible whenever you or your family need it.

Even people in the same family can be as different as neat-as-a-pin Felix and his devil-may-care buddy Oscar in Broadway's long-running play, *The Odd Couple*. Some of us immediately see the value of, and even enjoy, making orderly lists while others, no less in need of organization, find list-making tedious beyond endurance! Whichever tendency you relate to, we strongly encourage you to make use of the personal information lists. You might even find another family member to whom you could delegate the task—someone who would actually enjoy it!

Worth the Effort!

It's really not that hard to fill out the lists, and it is definitely worth the effort. We have found that the easiest way to record your own data on the lists is to chip away at the project.

For most of us, tackling all the lists at one time would be overwhelming. Instead, try sitting at a table or desk near your files with *Home Filing Made Easy!* propped open to whichever list you want to work on. Take out the related file, and open it up on the table. Fill in the spaces on the list, referring to the documents in your file as needed. If the necessary information is someplace else, now's the time to get it. Once you've entered it on the appropriate list, you'll always have it handy!

This Time Next Year

Even if you do only a couple of lists each month, before this time next year you will have an invaluable compendium of personal information at your fingertips. Time and time again you'll be glad that you made the effort to gather all this information onto your lists. They will make your HOMEFILE® system the unparalleled personal information system it was designed to be.

Tip: If you need more blank copies of the lists, make photocopies *before* you fill in your data. For example, you may want to have a Healthcare Providers list for each family member. It's also a great idea to keep a photocopy of your *completed* lists in your safe-deposit box. This can be an invaluable tool for supporting insurance claims after a fire or other casualty loss, and it will protect your investment of time in organizing all this valuable information.

Personal Information Lists*

Forms	Date Completed	Revision Date	2nd Revision Date
AUTOS			
BANK ACCOUNTS			
BOATS & RVs			
CREDIT CARDS			
HEALTHCARE PROVIDERS			
INSURANCE POLICIES			
INVESTMENT ACCOUNTS			
KEYS & SECURITY			
PERSONAL ADVISERS			
PERSONAL DATA			
REAL ESTATE BOUGHT & SOLD			
REAL ESTATE IMPROVEMENTS			
RELATIVES & CLERGY			
SAFE-DEPOSIT BOXES			
WILLS			

*Note: As you complete each list, jot down the date. Later, this will serve as a reminder that the information could be getting stale and may need revision. When you do update your list, make a note of the revision date.

Date: _____

AUTO 1

Year/Model	
Vehicle ID Number	
Purchased from	
Date Purchased	
Owner (Title)	
Insurance Company	
Date Sold	

AUTO 2

Year/Model	
Vehicle ID Number	
Purchased from	
Date Purchased	
Owner (Title)	
Insurance Company	
Date Sold	

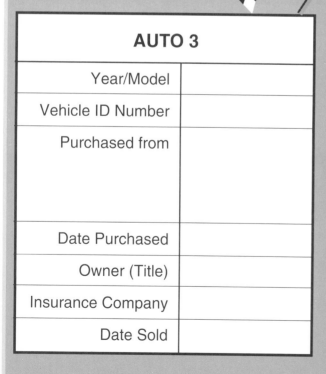

AUTO 3

Year/Model	
Vehicle ID Number	
Purchased from	
Date Purchased	
Owner (Title)	
Insurance Company	
Date Sold	

AUTO 4

Year/Model	
Vehicle ID Number	
Purchased from	
Date Purchased	
Owner (Title)	
Insurance Company	
Date Sold	

AUTOS

AUTO 5

Year/Model	
Vehicle ID Number	
Purchased from	
Date Purchased	
Owner (Title)	
Insurance Company	
Date Sold	

AUTO 6

Year/Model	
Vehicle ID Number	
Purchased from	
Date Purchased	
Owner (Title)	
Insurance Company	
Date Sold	

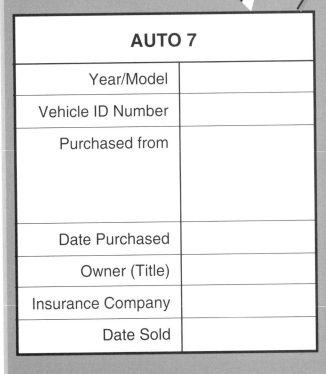

AUTO 7

Year/Model	
Vehicle ID Number	
Purchased from	
Date Purchased	
Owner (Title)	
Insurance Company	
Date Sold	

AUTO 8

Year/Model	
Vehicle ID Number	
Purchased from	
Date Purchased	
Owner (Title)	
Insurance Company	
Date Sold	

Date: _____

	ACCOUNT 1	ACCOUNT 2
Bank & Address		
Account #		
Type of Account		
Owner of Account		
Beneficiary of Account		
Contact Person/Phone		

	ACCOUNT 1	ACCOUNT 2
Bank & Address		
Account #		
Type of Account		
Owner of Account		
Beneficiary of Account		
Contact Person/Phone		

	ACCOUNT 1	ACCOUNT 2
Bank & Address		
Account #		
Type of Account		
Owner of Account		
Beneficiary of Account		
Contact Person/Phone		

Date: _____

BOAT/RV

Year/Model	
ID Number	
Purchased from	
Date Purchased	
Owner (Title)	
Insurance Company	
Date Sold	

BOAT/RV

Year/Model	
ID Number	
Purchased from	
Date Purchased	
Owner (Title)	
Insurance Company	
Date Sold	

BOAT/RV

Year/Model	
ID Number	
Purchased from	
Date Purchased	
Owner (Title)	
Insurance Company	
Date Sold	

BOAT/RV

Year/Model	
ID Number	
Purchased from	
Date Purchased	
Owner (Title)	
Insurance Company	
Date Sold	

Date: _____

	CREDIT CARD 1	**CREDIT CARD 2**
Type of Card	AMERICAN EXPRESS	DISCOVER NOVUS
Mailing Address		
Lost Card Phone #		
Inquiry Phone #		
Names of Cardholders		
Account #		
Max. Credit Line		

	CREDIT CARD 3	**CREDIT CARD 4**
Type of Card	MasterCard	VISA
Mailing Address		
Lost Card Phone #		
Inquiry Phone #		
Names of Cardholders		
Account #		
Max. Credit Line		

	CREDIT CARD 5	**CREDIT CARD 6**
Type of Card		
Mailing Address		
Lost Card Phone #		
Inquiry Phone #		
Names of Cardholders		
Account #		
Max. Credit Line		

	CREDIT CARD 7	CREDIT CARD 8
Type of Card		
Mailing Address		
Lost Card Phone #		
Inquiry Phone #		
Names of Cardholders		
Account #		
Max. Credit Line		

	CREDIT CARD 9	CREDIT CARD 10
Type of Card		
Mailing Address		
Lost Card Phone #		
Inquiry Phone #		
Names of Cardholders		
Account #		
Max. Credit Line		

	CREDIT CARD 11	CREDIT CARD 12
Type of Card		
Mailing Address		
Lost Card Phone #		
Inquiry Phone #		
Names of Cardholders		
Account #		
Max. Credit Line		

HEALTHCARE PROVIDERS

DOCTORS AND DENTISTS

Name	Specialty	Address/Phone #	Comments

EYEGLASSES, MEDICAL EQUIPMENT and DRUGSTORES

Doctor/Facility	Item Purchased	Address/Phone #	Comments

HOSPITALS, CLINICS, HMO FACILITIES, ETC.

Name of Institution	Specialty	Address/Phone #	Comments

INSURANCE POLICIES

Date: _____

Type of Policy	Name/Property Insured	Policy #	Insurance Co.	Agent/Address Phone #
Auto (1)				
Auto (2)				
Disability				
Excess Liability				
Health (1)				
Health (2)				
Home				
Life (1)				
Life (2)				
Life (3)				

Date: _____

Brokerage Firm	Personal Representative	Phone #	Account #
			1) _____ 2) _____ 3) _____
			1) _____ 2) _____ 3) _____
			1) _____ 2) _____ 3) _____

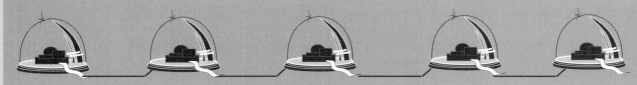

Mutual Funds	Personal Representative	Phone #	Account #
			1) _____ 2) _____ 3) _____
			1) _____ 2) _____ 3) _____
			1) _____ 2) _____ 3) _____

INVESTMENT ACCOUNTS 2

Date:_____

CD Issuer	Personal Representative	Phone #	Account #

Limited Partnerships	Personal Representative	Phone #	Account #

Other Active Investment Accounts	Personal Representative	Phone #	Account #

Date: _____

SPARE KEYS	LOCATIONS
Door	
Safe-Deposit Box	
Auto	
Boat/RV	
Storage Shed	
2nd House/Condo	
Other Property	
Security System	
Miscellaneous	

	SECURITY SYSTEM
Master Panel Location	
System Code #	
Emergency Phone #	
List of Other Relatives, Neighbors & Friends Who Have Spare Keys	
Procedure for Emergency	

PERSONAL ADVISERS

		ACCOUNTANT 1	ACCOUNTANT 2
	Name		
	Firm Name		
	Address		
	Work Phone #		
	Home Phone #		
	Matters Handled		

		ATTORNEY 1	ATTORNEY 2
	Name		
	Firm Name		
	Address		
	Work Phone #		
	Home Phone #		
	Matters Handled		

		FINANCIAL ADVISER 1	FINANCIAL ADVISER 2
	Name		
	Firm Name		
	Address		
	Work Phone #		
	Home Phone #		
	Matters Handled		

NOTE: Bankers, brokers, doctors, real estate and insurance agents are listed in their own sections.

PERSONAL DATA

Date: _____

FILL OUT A SEPARATE SHEET FOR EACH FAMILY MEMBER.	
Name of Family Member	
School, Work and/or Other Address/Phone #	
Close Friend's Name Address/Phone #	
Contact Person at Work	

Social Security #	
Driver's License #	
License Plate #	
Passport # / Expiration Date	
Bank Name	
Address	
Phone #	
Account #	
Credit Card #	

Physician's Name	
Physician's Phone #	
Blood Type	
Medical Allergies	
Special Medical Conditions	
Birthday	
Anniversary	
Other Information	

PERSONAL DATA

Date: _____

FILL OUT A SEPARATE SHEET FOR EACH FAMILY MEMBER.	
Name of Family Member	
School, Work and/or Other Address/Phone #	
Close Friend's Name Address/Phone #	
Contact Person at Work	

Social Security #	
Driver's License #	
License Plate #	
Passport # / Expiration Date	
Bank Name Address Phone # Account #	
Credit Card #	

Physician's Name	
Physician's Phone #	
Blood Type	
Medical Allergies	
Special Medical Conditions	
Birthday	
Anniversary	
Other Information	

PERSONAL DATA

Date: _____

FILL OUT A SEPARATE SHEET FOR EACH FAMILY MEMBER.	
Name of Family Member	
School, Work and/or Other Address/Phone #	
Close Friend's Name Address/Phone #	
Contact Person at Work	

Social Security #	
Driver's License #	
License Plate #	
Passport # / Expiration Date	
Bank Name	
Address	
Phone #	
Account #	
Credit Card #	

Physician's Name	
Physician's Phone #	
Blood Type	
Medical Allergies	
Special Medical Conditions	
Birthday	
Anniversary	
Other Information	

PERSONAL DATA

Date: _____

FILL OUT A SEPARATE SHEET FOR EACH FAMILY MEMBER.	
Name of Family Member	
School, Work and/or Other Address/Phone #	
Close Friend's Name Address/Phone #	
Contact Person at Work	

Social Security #	
Driver's License #	
License Plate #	
Passport # / Expiration Date	
Bank Name	
Address	
Phone #	
Account #	
Credit Card #	

Physician's Name	
Physician's Phone #	
Blood Type	
Medical Allergies	
Special Medical Conditions	
Birthday	
Anniversary	
Other Information	

PERSONAL DATA

Date: _____

FILL OUT A SEPARATE SHEET FOR EACH FAMILY MEMBER.

Name of Family Member	
School, Work and/or Other Address/Phone #	
Close Friend's Name Address/Phone #	
Contact Person at Work	

Social Security #	
Driver's License #	
License Plate #	
Passport # / Expiration Date	
Bank Name	
Address	
Phone #	
Account #	
Credit Card #	

Physician's Name	
Physician's Phone #	
Blood Type	
Medical Allergies	
Special Medical Conditions	
Birthday	
Anniversary	
Other Information	

PERSONAL DATA

Date:_____

FILL OUT A SEPARATE SHEET FOR EACH FAMILY MEMBER.	
Name of Family Member	
School, Work and/or Other Address/Phone #	
Close Friend's Name Address/Phone #	
Contact Person at Work	

Social Security #	
Driver's License #	
License Plate #	
Passport # / Expiration Date	
Bank　　　　Name	
Address	
Phone #	
Account #	
Credit Card #	

Physician's Name	
Physician's Phone #	
Blood Type	
Medical Allergies	
Special Medical Conditions	
Birthday	
Anniversary	
Other Information	

PROPERTY 1

Property	
Address	
Primary Residence?	☐ Yes ☐ No
Type of Property	
Owner (Title)	
Date Purchased	
Total Cost	
Date Sold	
Sale Proceeds	
Sales Agent/Agency	

PROPERTY 2

Property	
Address	
Primary Residence?	☐ Yes ☐ No
Type of Property	
Owner (Title)	
Date Purchased	
Total Cost	
Date Sold	
Sale Proceeds	
Sales Agent/Agency	

PROPERTY 3

Property	
Address	
Primary Residence?	☐ Yes ☐ No
Type of Property	
Owner (Title)	
Date Purchased	
Total Cost	
Date Sold	
Sale Proceeds	
Sales Agent/Agency	

PROPERTY 4

Property	
Address	
Primary Residence?	☐ Yes ☐ No
Type of Property	
Owner (Title)	
Date Purchased	
Total Cost	
Date Sold	
Sale Proceeds	
Sales Agent/Agency	

	FILL OUT A SEPARATE LIST FOR EACH PROPERTY.			
PROPERTY	NATURE OF IMPROVEMENT		DATE	COST

NOTE: File receipts in "Active: Residence" or "Active: Real Estate."

REAL ESTATE Improvements

Date: _____

PROPERTY	NATURE OF IMPROVEMENT		DATE	COST

FILL OUT A SEPARATE LIST FOR EACH PROPERTY.

NOTE: File receipts in "Active: Residence" or "Active: Real Estate."

RELATIVES & CLERGY

HELPFUL FOR MAKING CONTACT IN EMERGENCIES

	PARENT	PARENT
Name		
Address		
Phone #		
Whose Parents?		
	CHILD	**CHILD**
Name		
Address		
Phone #		
Whose Child?		
	OTHER FAMILY MEMBER	**OTHER FAMILY MEMBER**
Name		
Address		
Phone #		
Whose Sibling?		
	CLERGY	**CLERGY**
Name		
Church		
Address / Phone #		
	NEIGHBOR	**NEIGHBOR**
Name		
Address		
Phone #		

SAFE-DEPOSIT BOXES

Date: _____

BANK	
Address	
Phone #	
Box #	
Authorized Person	

BANK	
Address	
Phone #	
Box #	
Authorized Person	

CONTENTS

CONTENTS

Date: _____

INFORMATION ON PERSONAL WILLS

Whose Will?	
Will Drawn by	
Date of Original Will	
Date Last Reviewed	
Codicil / Date Added	
Executor (Personal Representative)	
Address / Phone #	
Location of Will	

Whose Will?	
Will Drawn by	
Date of Original Will	
Date Last Reviewed	
Codicil / Date Added	
Executor (Personal Representative)	
Address / Phone #	
Location of Will	

Whose Will?	
Will Drawn by	
Date of Original Will	
Date Last Reviewed	
Codicil / Date Added	
Executor (Personal Representative)	
Address / Phone #	
Location of Will	

Cash Management

An efficient cash management system is indispensable to achieving a sense of financial well-being. The only way most of us will ever have money left over for long-term goals like college funding and retirement is to divert a certain amount of our current income into savings before we have the chance to spend it. The economic textbook definition of *savings* is "postponed consumption"; not very many of us are naturally good at it! To develop a skill for saving, we need clear goals (to provide the incentive) and a smoothly functioning routine for staying in control of our income and outgo. A bill-paying system, a spending plan, a saving plan and an efficient recordkeeping system are all essential components of a personal cash management system.

Bill-paying has a kind of life of its own, so it needs to operate separately from the rest of your personal recordkeeping. That is why we have not made a regular file category for bills. Ultimately, though, your bill-paying routine and your filing system *do* need to work together. For example, when your monthly bank statement arrives, you will want to keep it with your bill-paying records until you have had a chance to reconcile it with your checkbook; *then* it can go into your "Bank Accounts" file.

Precious few of us actually *enjoy* paying bills. Many people, in fact, find it a more frustrating experience than it needs to be. Like so many other things in life, paying bills becomes much more manageable when you break the chore into little steps. That's what this chapter is really about: organizing the whole bill-paying process into an eight-step routine that you can repeat effortlessly month after month.

Why Is Bill-Paying
So Complicated ?

As we reflect back on the 1940s and 1950s, it seems that household financial management was a simpler task for Mom and Dad than it is for today's families. They wrote a lot fewer checks, probably did not have car payments, never owned a credit card and had very basic tax records. They knew what they could and couldn't afford by looking at their bank balance!

Today, of course, "afford" has an entirely different meaning to many folks, often defined by "what are the monthly payments?" As a society, we don't save very well; we live closer to the edge than our forebears. If that were not stressful enough, our daily mail brings us reminders of car loan payments, car insurance premiums, invoices for life insurance and health insurance, utilities, doctor bills, mortgage or rent notices, and several credit card statements looking for "minimum payments." Even our formerly simple phone bill now comes from different companies for long distance and local calls!

Some bills are for predictable amounts while some are irregular; still others offer flexible terms—pay me now or pay me later. Most bills appear in our mailbox *monthly*, but some are on a *quarterly* or *annual* cycle. This means that in many households, the monthly cash demands are irregular and hard to predict.

The availability of credit is so great and the list of bills so long that the typical American family is actually spending more than its income year after year! The household that can pay all its accounts monthly is becoming more the exception than the rule. When we throw in the increasing incidence of job loss and career insecurity, it is easy to understand why bill paying has become not only complicated but stressful as well.

Bill-Paying 101

Following this simple, eight-step ritual will eliminate unnecessary overdue notices. It will reduce the actual time you spend processing your personal bills. It will help eliminate unwitting check account overdrafts. It will even help you build a database for budgeting.

Step 1
File Incoming Bills

You will want to start by setting up 12 files, one labeled for each month of the year. Next, establish three more files with the following category titles:

- Bills To Pay
- Checking Accounts
- Credit Cards

As bills arrive in the daily mail, you can just stash them in the file marked "Bills To Pay." If you are in a hurry, you don't need to open them right away. At least you'll have them separated from the ad flyers, catalogs and solicitations, so you won't lose them!

If you do have a minute, open the envelope and at least glance at the bill before placing it in the folder. This way you can be sure whether there are any surprises that need immediate attention. For example, if your credit card statement shows that you exceeded your credit limit, you'll want to take care of that before you offer your card for that next car rental or plane ticket! If you have gotten behind on your electric bill because you've been out of town, a shutoff notice could be attached to your invoice—you would probably prefer to know about this *before* it happens so you can head it off!

Step 2
Dedicate a
Specific Time

Decide on at least one *specific* time in the month that you will dedicate to paying current bills. Be very strict about preserving this time from other demands. Having your bills paid on time brings a lot of peace into your life, so it is worth sticking to a schedule. A particular weekday evening is a popular choice. For other households, a morning time slot might work better. Or maybe you'd prefer an hour on Saturday. Decide what is best for you, and stick to it.

Many folks find that it is actually better to pay bills twice a month, making it a shorter task each time. Not all bills fall due the same day, of course, so having two sessions can help avoid unnecessary interest charges or late fees.

Whether you pay once, twice or four times a month, use the same bill-paying worksheet for the whole month; just add new bills to the list each time. If you have a really busy household with more bills than you can fit on a single worksheet, simply use two worksheets for a single month (more about worksheets in Step 5).

Step 3
Gather Your Supplies

Nothing is more frustrating than getting all settled down to a task and then having to jump up to find a pen, address label, stamp or envelope. (The BILL PAYER™ by HOMEFILE® includes the BILL PAYER™ CADDY, which holds most of the little things you tend to forget. See order information at the back of this book.) Here's a checklist to help you be sure that you have everything you need before you start:

- Bill-Paying Worksheet (see page 142)
- Calculator
- Checkbook
- Envelopes
- Pencil or pen
- Postage stamps
- Return address stickers or stamper
- Stapler

Step 4
Stack 'Em Up,
Look 'Em Over

When you are ready to start, take your bills out of the "Bills To Pay" folder. If you haven't already done so, remove all the outer envelopes and throw them away (unless they are part of the return mail envelope). Make a stack of the bills along with their payment envelopes if they are provided.

Look over each bill for accuracy. For example, occasionally we'll get a bill that isn't ours. If that happens to you, just put it aside and deal with it when you're finished with your *real* bills. Or sometimes our payment of last month's bill crosses in the mail with this month's notice. When that happens, the new one will show two payments due! To be sure that you have already paid it (or to check if you are unsure), just pull the last month's file folder, and look at the worksheet to see if it *was* paid. If it was, note that on the new invoice, and put it back on the stack of bills.

Step 5
Make a List

Figure 7.1 shows a copy of the BILL PAYER™ Monthly Worksheet; use this to make photocopies for your own use. Put one copy in each of your 12 monthly files so that you will have a whole year's supply on hand. On this worksheet, list all the bills you have in the stack (Step 4). If you follow the worksheet column headings, you will capture a lot of information about each bill, including the amount owed, when it is due and the minimum payment required. You will be able to fill in the number of the check you use to pay each bill, the date you pay it and, if you keep such records, the expense category you have assigned to that item.

Expense categories are useful for keeping track of how much you spend on different items like car insurance or eating out. You can look back over a period of time to see how you are actually spending your income; in turn, this knowledge is valuable for forecasting your living expenses and for making spending decisions or a *spending plan*. A spending plan is almost a necessity during times of important change in a person's or family's financial life, such as marriage, empty nest time and retirement. If you have a computer, you can choose from several easy-to-use programs for this purpose; the expense category numbers on your worksheet can be transferred to such a program.

Figure 7.1 BILLPAYER™ *Monthly Worksheet*

BILLPAYER™ **Monthly Worksheet**   Month/ Yr. _____

Due Date	Category #	Check #	Bill Owed	Min. $ Payment	$ Amount Paid	Date Paid
TOTAL						

Figure 7.2 below shows a sample worksheet filled in with one family's bills to serve as a model for you to follow.

Figure 7.2 Sample Worksheet

BILLPAYER™ Monthly Worksheet   Month/ Yr. _____

Due Date	Category #	Check #	Bill Owed	Min. $ Payment	$ Amount Paid	Date Paid
4/22	202	345	Gas & Electric Co.	145	145	4/16
4/17	333	346	Local Phone Co.	30	30	4/16
4/19	333	347	Long Distance Co.	201	201	4/16
4/29	234	348	Gas Card	112	112	4/16
4/15	202	349	Water bill	145	145	4/16
4/07	202	350	Heating Oil Co.	120	120	4/16
4/12	141	351	Mortgage Co.	1500	1500	4/16
4/28	111	352	Book Club	25	25	4/16

©1993 Financial Advantage, Inc.

Step 6
Prioritize Your Bills

When you have listed all the bills on the worksheet, total up the column marked "Minimum Payment Due." Or if you know you are going to make different payments, fill in the blanks in the column marked "Amount Paid" and total these.

Now it's time to compare the total bills due with the cash available. Usually this is in the checking account that you use for household bills. If there's plenty of cash, go ahead and pay them all! (Make sure that you leave enough cash to meet your out-of-pocket or other spending needs that will come up before the next deposit.) If cash is short, you need to *prioritize your bills* and decide which ones to pay first. Separate the bills you are NOT going to pay right now and return them to the "Bills To Pay" folder. That leaves you with a stack of bills you are going to pay now.

Prioritizing Tips.   There are as many different situations as there are households, so we can't offer advice for every eventuality. However, here are a few guidelines for prioritizing.

Look at the due dates.   If you can pay the oldest bills first, will that get you to the next bill-paying session without any overdue notices?

Which bills will cost you interest or penalties if you pay them later? Sometimes this is a valid way to decide on paying priorities.

Many doctors and others have recently begun to tack late fees onto bills, so take a close look.

Some bills have more serious penalties for lateness than just interest charges . . . like shutting off your phone or electric power, putting a blemish on your credit record or foreclosing on your mortgage! If your household gets into a serious cash bind, these may be the more important ways to prioritize bills until you can catch up.

Note: If you are already in this situation like many families today, you probably realize that these are serious warning signs. You definitely need to make a plan for cutting expenses, increasing income or both. If you are not sure how to do that, find an adviser who can help. In most metropolitan areas, Consumer Credit Counseling Services (CCCS) can help for little or no charge; look in the *Yellow Pages*. State Extension Services have good materials, too. For a biblical perspective on finances and getting out of debt, you might call Christian Financial Concepts (Larry Burkett's well-known organization) for information about seminars or counselors near you at 404-534-1000.

Tip: *Consider partial payments where necessary;* creditors are generally much happier to see a partial payment with a note or phone call from you than to be totally ignored. So when you're in a bind, *contact* your creditors—don't stick your head in the sand and hope they'll go away. They won't!

Step 7
Write the Checks!

Now, you've listed all your bills, calculated the total amount you owe and decided which bills you are going to pay at this sitting.

Pick up the first bill in your stack, and write your check to that creditor for the amount due (or for the amount that you have decided to pay). Don't forget to fill in your checkbook stub or register along with each check. Also, it's a good idea, sometimes even a requirement from the creditor, to write the account number or invoice number on the memo portion of your check in case it gets separated from your payment slip when it's being processed.

Jot the check number next to that bill on your monthly worksheet. Place your check and whatever payment slip goes with it into the return envelope. If none is provided, use your own 6¾-inch security envelope (the kind you can't see through). Write the address on it NOW, before you seal it up with your only copy of the address inside!

Put the completed envelope off to one side to be stamped later. If you have some kind of receipt or bill stub left, put that off to the other side; when you've finished, these receipts will be returned to the monthly file folder as a record.

Follow this same procedure with each bill until you have finished off the whole stack!

Step 8
The Envelope, Please

Now, all your checks are written and recorded in the checkbook and on the monthly worksheet. Next, you can tackle the pile of envelopes you've created. Seal them, place a first-class stamp on the ones that require it and put a return address with either a sticker or an inked stamp. Drop them in the nearest U.S. mailbox, and leave the rest to the post office.

Whew! Feeling the satisfaction of a job well done, you can put everything away until next month (or the next bill-paying session). Fold your monthly worksheet in half, and put inside it or staple to it that little pile of bill receipts you just collected. Put it back in its monthly file folder. All that information will be available if you need to refer to it in the future.

No doubt, tomorrow's mail will bring another new bill. Pop it into the "Bills To Pay" folder, and the cycle starts all over again!

Managing Your Credit Cards

Annual charge volume has been growing at a double-digit pace. American consumers charged nearly $400 billion on their general-purpose credit cards in 1993!

Charge plates (store-specific credit cards) came into widespread use in the 1950s as a convenience to shoppers and as a way of spreading out payments on large purchases such as furniture. General purpose credit cards, though, are a fairly recent phenomenon. In the 1950s, such cards were offered only to business people and the well-to-do for travel and dining. It wasn't long before the banks saw an opportunity to preapprove credit for average citizens and offer them the use-it-anywhere plastic money. Computers made it increasingly easy to keep track of billions of transactions, and in no time at all, most adult Americans found themselves with a wallet full of plastic buying power… and the need to record and control its use.

Keeping Track of Credit Receipts

Have you ever scanned your monthly credit card statement and found that something you didn't recognize was charged to your account? How many times have you wanted to return an item but couldn't find your copy of the receipt? How about the exasperated feeling you had of seeing a dresser top cluttered with dozens of those impossible-to-read printouts; do you need them, or can you throw them away?

If you use your credit cards often, staying on top of all the receipts and statements can seem overwhelming. We offer you this simple method for keeping it under control.

Each time you make an in-person purchase using a credit card, you should receive a paper receipt with your card number, the date, vendor name and details of the purchase. (If you don't, be sure to insist on it.) This is usually a flimsy, hard-to-read document, but it's more valuable than it may appear to be. Hang on to it.

The system that seems to work best is to make a little agreement with yourself that every night you will unload all receipts from your pockets, wallet, purse or wherever you stash them. In a convenient place, keep a small box or a large manila envelope marked "Credit Receipts." Put all your receipts in this container *every* night. Then, even if you do nothing else, you should be able to find one of these receipts if you absolutely need it. (HOMEFILE® publishes a complete bill-paying system with a bill caddy for holding all these records; for information about the BILLPAYER™ by HOMEFILE®, see the form at the back of this book.)

Why do you need a credit transaction receipt? Well, you can check whether that mysterious charge on your statement was put there by mistake or is a purchase you had simply forgotten. If the new clock radio stops keeping time while it is under warranty, you'll have the necessary proof of purchase. Did you charge a hotel bill or a dinner for business purposes? It's necessary to have a receipt in case the IRS wants to see it.

When you sit down to pay bills, that's a perfect time to pull out the credit receipts and compare them with your monthly credit card statement. If you have receipts for purchases that haven't appeared yet, leave them in the envelope until they do show up on a monthly statement. Are there items on your statement you don't recognize and don't have a receipt for? Don't hesitate to notify the card issuer about it; mistakes do happen, but they don't have to cost you money! *Most monthly statements have information printed on the back about how to dispute a charge.*

What do you do with the other receipts, the ones that correctly match up with your statement? Save them if they fall into one of these categories:

- Evidence of important purchase or cost
- Receipt for warranted purchase
- Tax-related expenditure

Most credit card purchases that don't fit one of these categories are just routine outlays. You probably don't need them after they show up on your statement. To be conservative, take each month's receipts that don't fall into one of the three categories above, and put them into an envelope marked with the month and year. Save them in a file, drawer or shoe box, and throw them away when they are one year old.

For those receipts you *do* want to retain, file them in the appropriate HOMEFILE® category to make them easier to retrieve if you ever need them.

Monthly Credit Card Statements

When your monthly credit card statement arrives in the mail, you can store it in the hanging file labeled "Bills To Pay" until you're ready to deal with it. As with any bill, it is a good idea to open the outer envelope and glance at the statement before placing it in the folder...just to be sure there are no surprises that need immediate attention. For example, you don't want to ignore a credit card that's over its limit! Rember to throw away the outer envelope. This will save you time later when you are ready to process your bills. It will also keep your "Bills To Pay" folder uncluttered.

How long should you save the monthly credit card statement? We suggest keeping it in the monthly bill file and disposing of it after a year. The individual purchase receipts (not the monthly statements) will be your evidence of transactions for tax and other reasons; those are the more important papers for tax purposes.

Balancing Your Checkbook

A Chore Worth Doing

A surprising number of us are so intimidated by the prospect of balancing our checkbooks that we actually never do it! We are content to take the bank's word for how much money we have spent and how much is left. But banks *do make mistakes*—and possibly not always in our favor!

You receive several benefits from reviewing your checking activity monthly. First, of course, you can verify whether every deduction from your account is one that you authorized. Second, you discover whether you actually have as much money left as you thought you did (if you had any idea at all!). Such knowledge will save you the embarrassment and expense of writing checks that exceed your available balance. A third benefit of monthly review is that you become more familiar with your own spending patterns (e.g., "I didn't realize I spent so much at the butcher's."). This will help you make spending decisions that result in more satisfaction even if you don't work from a formal budget.

Lack of time is a commonly offered excuse for not matching our checkbook with the bank's statement. In this chapter, we reduce the task to a simple, repeatable process that *you can accomplish in less than 30 minutes* each month. Isn't it worth one minute a day to *know* how much you have in your checking account, to *know* where all your money is going and to *know* you'll never bounce another check? (Avoiding one bounced-check fee a month is like earning $1 a minute!)

Essentials of the Process

Euclid unlocked the mysteries of geometry by reducing observed patterns to their simplest components. Our personal finances can benefit from the same approach, so we hope you won't be offended if our explanation of the checking account process seems too basic. *Here's how it works:*

How checking works. You allow a bank to hold your money until it receives a written authorization from you to release a portion of it to someone whom you name. That authorization, of course, is your check.

Every month, the bank reports to you all transactions in which they paid money out of your account. The same report also shows any new money that was deposited into your account during the month. This report or *statement* is the bank's way of being accountable to you.

The conclusion of the report is one simple number—how much money was left in your account on the last day of the period.

Why you need parallel records. Each time you write a check, you make your own record of it on your checkbook stub or register. Whenever you deposit new money into your account, the bank gives you a receipt for that amount; they record it in their computer, and you write it in your checkbook.

The reason for these parallel records (yours and the bank's) is to ensure that you get credit for every dollar you put in and that no money goes out without your authorization. *It enhances accuracy and prevents fraud IF YOU CHECK the bank's records against your own.*

Balancing your checkbook. So *balancing your checkbook* is really a process of comparing your records with the bank's and bringing up-to-date your cash balance so that you know what you have. Keep in mind a couple of basics:

The bank's monthly report to you can include only checks that have been presented to it for payment. Usually there are at least a few checks that you have written but that have not yet been presented to the bank. In a similar fashion, *there is often a time lag between when you make a deposit and when the money is actually available to your account,* such as when you deposit an out-of-town check. So *your* records may show a check or a deposit that the bank is not yet able to show on *its* report. When you compare records, you need to take this into account to be accurate. It's easy; we'll show you how!

In addition to checks, there are a few other ways that money can legitimately find its way out of your checking account. You might make cash withdrawals from an *automated teller machine* (ATM). The bank may charge service fees, and there may be regular withdrawals that you have preauthorized, such as car payments or health club dues. Your recordkeeping routine needs to encompass all of these to ensure their accuracy.

Six Easy Steps

When your monthly checking account statement arrives in the mail, store it in the file labeled, "Checking Accounts." Plan on using it to balance your checkbook sometime during the month, perhaps at the same time you sit down to pay bills. To update your checkbook balance and protect yourself from error or fraud each month, follow these six easy steps:

1. *Arrange canceled checks by check number.* Go through the pile, marking each one of them in your check register or "stub book" so you know which ones have cleared your account. We suggest using a colored highlighter pen to mark the returned-check numbers in your checkbook.

2. *Go through the pile of canceled checks again—this time, compare the amount of each check with the entries on the bank statement.* Highlight or mark each bank entry that matches a check amount. When you are finished, every withdrawal on the bank's list should be marked. Any that are not marked should be a bank fee, ATM transaction or preauthorized withdrawal. If anything does not match up, call your bank right away to get it cleared up!

3. *Update your own checkbook balance by subtracting any fees or preauthorized withdrawals that you have not yet entered.* Also, compare the *deposits* entered in your book with those the bank credited to you. If you have forgotten to write in any or if you earned interest credits, *add* these to your checkbook balance now.

4. Write down the following information; either make photo-copies of this format, or use the one on the reverse of your monthly bank statement.

    A. List *deposits* or credits that appear in *your* checkbook but do NOT appear in the bank statement.

	Check #	$ Amount
	_____	_____
	_____	_____
	_____	_____
Deposit Subtotal		_____

    B. List *withdrawals* (checks, preauthorized or ATMs) that appear in your checkbook but do NOT appear in the bank statement. *(Save ATM receipts during the month; if you haven't recorded ATM transactions in checkbook, refer to your receipts.)*

	Check #	$ Amount
	_____	_____
	_____	_____
	_____	_____
	_____	_____
	_____	_____
	_____	_____
	_____	_____
	_____	_____
	_____	_____
	_____	_____
	_____	_____
Withdrawal Subtotal		_____

5. Enter final *balance* from bank *statement.* _____

    Add total from item 4A (above). + _____

                          Subtotal _____

    Subtract subtotal from 4B (above). – _____

              GRAND TOTAL _____

Troubleshooting

6. If the grand total matches your checkbook balance, you have successfully balanced your checkbook! If NOT, see below.

   a) Examine your checkbook register for math errors.

   b) Did you record every transaction? If you hold a joint account, did you *both* record every transaction? What about uncleared checks and ones still outstanding from the *last* statement?

   c) Look for transfers, e.g., checking to savings account.

   d) Still have a discrepancy? Call your bank for assistance or correction.

So there you have it, the three essential parts of the bill-paying routine:

- Paying the bills
- Checking the credit card statements
- Balancing your checkbook

When you have filed your important papers in order and paid your bills on time, you will experience a new level of personal satisfaction and peace that flow from having control over your own life. In Chapter 10, we'll put a ribbon on the package by offering some tips for organizing some of the nonfinancial "stuff" than you probably save.

Part III

Related Topics

Part III

Part III

Part III

Part III

Part III

Part III

Part III

Part III

Part III

The Safety Factor and Your Files!

8

Kinds of Disasters That Can Affect Your Important Papers

Before we met Barbara, she was pleased with her life as a full-time homemaker and mother of five. Her husband, Jim, was a rising mid-level executive at a large company. When we met her, she was working full-time in a local bank, and Jim was selling ice cream from a jingle-bell truck 13 hours a day! Why all the change? They were working desperately to generate cash to rebuild their home, which was destroyed by fire while they were on vacation. Sadly, their home had become under-insured due to inflation of its value; they had lost everything. Barbara's story permanently influenced our attitude toward risk.

Newspapers daily report a litany of disasters that damage, destroy and snatch away not only people's property but their valuable records as well. You probably take time to have good insurance protection for your property, but do you make an effort to keep your records safe from fire, flood and theft? If you lose your files, you'll suffer grief and frustration and pay a high price in time and money trying to reconstruct them.

Here are just a few catastrophes to keep in mind:

- "Natural" disasters such as floods, hurricanes, tornados, earthquakes, etc.

- Other disasters, such as plumbing and gas leaks, power failures, bomb explosions and fires

- Malicious interference, such as theft and vandalism

- And, of course, some disasters that are the consequences of our own carelessness. Life can be so hectic today that it is very common for valuable papers to "get lost."

Protecting Valuable Papers from Potential Disasters

Safe-Deposit Boxes: Factors To Consider

Opinions vary widely about the advantages and disadvantages of using a bank's safe-deposit box for storing valuables.

Protection.   The obvious purpose is to provide *maximum* protection against the risks of fire and theft.

Privacy.   Strict privacy is another important feature.

Cost.   In return for these benefits, you have to be willing to pay a price, of course. The depository institution charges an annual fee that depends on the size of the box you rent. A typical small box measures 2" x 5" x 24", and the cost ranges upwards from about $20 a year.

Access and convenience.   There is also the convenience factor to be considered—your access to the box is probably limited to business hours. Limited access requires a little planning on your part when you need to retrieve items from the safe-deposit box. Your own preference depends on whether a safe-deposit box at a bank or other institution provides enough convenient access for you and also on whether you have a secure alternative for your valuables, such as a fireproof safe in your home or office.

Helpful Equipment for Safekeeping Valuables at Home or Office

A fireproof safe. A fireproof safe at home is a good indication of your prudence. You can find many varieties on the market, including a small portable fireproof "suitcase" that can be carried out in case of fire. One- and two-drawer fireproof filing cabinets are also available. Prices have become very reasonable—ask anyone who has experienced a fire what it would have been worth to them to have their valuable papers restored! See the "Source Guide" section in the back of this book for the names of manufacturers who make these files.

Locks. Most file cabinets are available with locks; ask your office supply dealer for more information, or call a local locksmith who can install a file cabinet lock for you.

A security system. A security system for your home certainly protects your valuable papers as well as your home. An audible alarm is a great deterrent to most thieves.

Fire extinguishers and smoke/heat detectors. Make sure that you place them where you store your records in addition to the other areas in your home recommended by fire departments.

Safes to protect computerized data on disks. If you have important data on computer disks, store them in a special fireproof safe that protects computer disks. Disks are even less tolerant of heat than papers are, so the fireproof container needs to be designed to protect them from heat as well as fire. Special inserts for putting computer and other electronic storage items into ordinary fireproof safes are also available.

What Are "Valuables"?

No list could ever include all the items that every person might own that should be kept in a "safe" place. The following list represents the kinds of things people tend to store in their safe-deposit boxes. Create your own list, and check with your accountant and your lawyer to be sure that all the things that are important to *your* circumstances are included in your list.

Originals and Copies of Valuable Documents and Other Legal Papers

- Adoption, child custody or guardianship papers

- Baptismal and other religious certificates

- Birth and death certificates

- Deeds, titles and other records of ownership

- Leases

- Military documents

- Naturalization or alien registration records

- Papers concerning marriage, separation or divorce

- Passports

- Powers of attorney

- Real estate deeds

- Stocks, bonds and other investment certificates

- Trusts

- Add your own. _____

  _____

Personal Property Inventory
for Insurance Purposes

It is hard to exaggerate the importance of a written inventory of your possessions. When people lose their homes, it is almost impossible for them to remember all the items buried in that charred pile of rubble. A house fire is an emotionally wrenching experience and is *not* the time to be trying to list all the possessions that are now gone. Having appropriate supporting information can make all the difference in negotiating an adequate insurance settlement.

For your inventory, you will need to gather information from each property you occupy. Don't forget to include cars and equipment you own, such as recreational vehicles or boats, and items in your garages, sheds or a storage warehouse. Here are suggestions on what to include in your inventory.

Description of possessions. It's a good idea to go from room to room as you write your list. First note major items of furniture, appliances and equipment as well as valuable decorations and collectibles; then check drawers and cabinets for valuables that may be inside. Don't forget the obvious things such as carpeting, draperies and pictures—these types of things become an almost indistinguishable part of the room, and you can forget they are separate items of value.

Major appliances. List the model number, year purchased, brand name and cost for each major appliance, computer and electronic item.

Photographs or videotapes. Photos or videotapes showing the condition and quality of your valuables are an excellent idea. Some photographers even specialize in this type of work.

Appraisals of expensive items. These items include antiques, artwork, furs, jewelry and collectibles. Keep the original appraisal in your safe-deposit box and a copy with your homeowners policy, where they are listed as "scheduled" items. Remember to check with your insurance agent if you have any questions concerning the coverage of any of these items. *Don't* assume your possessions are properly covered; ask your agent to be sure.

Sales receipts. Sales receipts help establish the value of your more expensive belongings.

Whether you rent or own your home, be sure to review your insurance coverages annually, and keep coverage current with today's replacement costs.

Lists of Insurance Policies and Their Numbers

You can keep actual insurance policies at home and a copy in your safe-deposit box; insurance companies will replace policies whenever necessary. See the four insurance category descriptions in Chapter 3 for more information about the types of insurance records you need to keep. After you have filled out your insurance policies list in Chapter 6, you will have in one place all your important policy numbers, agents' names and phone numbers. *Make a copy of this sheet to keep in your safe-deposit box.* It will be an invaluable aid if any loss occurs.

Infrequently Accessed Valuables

Because some valuables are used only infrequently, you might easily forget about them in the wake of a traumatic loss. It might be years before you remember that you owned them . . . too late to file an insurance claim. These could include the following items:

- Seldom-worn, expensive jewelry

- Family heirlooms infrequently used and irreplaceable

- Gold and/or rare coins

- Stamps and other valuable collections. If you keep your collections elsewhere, it would be an excellent idea to document in your safe-deposit box what these items or collections are, their value and current location.

- Negatives of treasured family photos

- Add your own infrequently used valuables here.

_____

Photocopy of All HOMEFILE® Lists

• One of the best ways we know to capture the information that floats around our lives is by using the HOMEFILE® personal information lists in Chapter 6, "Data Collection Center." Once you have completed these worksheets with your own valuable data, make a copy of each form, and keep them in your safe-deposit box.

Safe Locations for Your Will

••Warning••

DO NOT KEEP WILLS IN SAFE-DEPOSIT BOX.

Most states provide that a person's safe-deposit box cannot be opened after his or her death except in the presence of a tax agent or until an executor or administrator has been appointed by the court. Ask your bank what their rules and your state's regulations are. Losing a friend or family member is traumatic enough; you don't want to add unnecessary complications by having their final instructions locked up in a safe-deposit box that no one is authorized to open!

The generic wisdom for the safekeeping of a will is to put it where:

1. it is secure from fire, flood, theft and unauthorized readers and

2. your personal representative (executor) knows of its location.

Where Can You Keep Your Will Safe?

The following are examples of ways to store your estate documents so that they will be safe and accessible.

A fireproof safe in your own home. Be sure that your personal representative knows of the location and has access to the key or combination.

The registrar of wills in the jurisdiction where you reside. For a nominal fee, you can physically file your will with the court system; you can retrieve it whenever you want. It is a good idea to write your Social Security number and the identity of your personal representative right on the cover.

With your attorney. Some attorneys are willing to store the originals of their clients' wills; however, most seem to prefer that each person take responsibility for his or her own. Lawyers usually keep a *conformed* copy and can use that to prepare a new original if yours is lost or destroyed. *(Note: Technically, only originals are accepted by courts.)*

The IRS and Your Files!

The Annual Ritual

Sometime between New Year's Day and April 15, most Americans must tackle the monumental task of gathering data to prepare their tax return for the Internal Revenue Service (IRS). Whether you prepare your own tax return or rely on a professional to complete the confusing forms, *you* are the one who must unearth all the income records and find the receipts that will document all your deductions. Every April 15, TV evening news crews station themselves at post offices in cities and towns throughout the country to record long lines of citizens rushing to meet the midnight filing deadline. This ritual bears witness to our procrastination in the face of such an unpleasant task. Simplifying the annual tax record search may be the greatest benefit of the HOMEFILE® system. It will save you time, reduce frustration and save you money by helping you get every deduction you deserve!

Recommended Process

During the year, you will have sorted lots of information by category (Blue Cross records in the "Insurance (Health)" file, etc.). At tax time, however, much of your data takes on a whole new significance! The information that you need for the IRS will be spread among many of your current files. Our staff recommends the following process as a workable way to assemble all your data for the Big Day.

Begin the annual ritual by sifting through the current year's documents in each of the files we have listed on the next page. Your purpose is two-fold. Look first for records of *taxable income,* such as wages, salary, interest and dividends. Then sort through the files for evidence of those precious and increasingly rare *deductible expenditures,* such as mortgage interest, medical outlays and charitable contributions.

Gather all these essential documents into two piles: one for income and one for deductions. As you wade through your tax forms or your tax preparer's information form, you will be able to find the necessary records in these two piles. Most people find it easier to comb through all their files at the beginning of the process than to conduct a file search every time the tax forms call for another piece of data.

Canceled checks are a key source of tax-time information. If you have been diligent during the year in putting your tax-related canceled checks into the right files, you will discover them when you go through the files to gather your *deduction* records. Nevertheless, our experience is that it's a good idea to leaf through your **whole year's checkbook register** anyway. Look for potentially deductible outlays that you may not have segregated into files during the year. This way, you can be more certain not to miss any deductions that you are entitled to. The accountant or tax preparer who is familiar with your personal situation can give you a definitive list of what to look for.

As you do the gleaning work for your tax preparation, you can be accomplishing two things at once: assembling the current data for your tax return and selecting those items that you will be moving to the archive files. (*See* Chapter 4, "The Quick-Find Index," and the "When To Remove" section of the file category descriptions.)

Income Categories

The following files usually contain *Income Items:*

BANK ACCOUNTS
EMPLOYMENT
INSURANCE (Life & Annuity)
INVESTMENTS
REAL ESTATE
RETIREMENT SAVINGS
SELF-EMPLOYED
SOCIAL SECURITY
TAXES (Income)
WILLS & TRUSTS

Deductions Categories

The following files usually contain *Deductions:*

CHARITIES
CREDIT
EXPENSES (Employment & Misc.)
INSURANCE (all four types)
INVESTMENTS
MEDICAL RECORDS
REAL ESTATE
RESIDENCE
RETIREMENT SAVINGS
SCHOOLS & CHILDCARE
SELF-EMPLOYED
TAXES (Income)

Keep a Copy

Once your tax return is completed, make a copy *before* sending it to the tax authorities. Then fasten to your copy of the return all the supporting documents; the burden of proof is on you to produce these records if asked.

Tip: Another practical way we have discovered for keeping each year's documents and worksheets together with the tax return is to put them all into a plastic food storage bag and keep it in your file! When you need to access an old tax return, you can read through the bag to tell at a glance if it contains the records for the year you need! Store this package in your "Taxes (Income)" file. Take the previous year's return out of this current file, and move it to "Archive: Taxes (Income)."

How Long Must You Keep Tax Records?

Perhaps the question we are asked most frequently is, "How long must I keep my tax records?" The specific rules are a little tricky, and it is worth asking your tax adviser. However, a few general guidelines may be helpful.

The IRS has *three years* to raise routine questions about your tax return, *six years* if it thinks you substantially underreported income. In cases of fraud, there is no time limitation on the government's right to inquire. Based on these guidelines, tax advisers usually recommend keeping records at least six years.

However, there are reasons for keeping some kinds of tax records much longer than the general six-year rule. In many cases, the category descriptions explain these rules under the heading, "When To Remove." For example, you will find recordkeeping rules that relate to retirement savings and to capital gains from the sale of your residence, real estate or other investments in the category descriptions. This is another area where you may want to consult with your accountant or tax preparer.

Some of your expenses may be either tax deductible or nondeductible depending on a variety of factors. You can check with the IRS publications listed on the next page and find most of the answers you are looking for—they are free! You can order these publications from the IRS, or you can read or photocopy them at many public libraries. Ask for IRS Publication #920 for a complete list of available publications.

Pub. #	Title
1	Your Rights as a Taxpayer
2	The ABC's of Income Tax
17	Your Federal Income Tax
463	Travel, Entertainment and Gift Deductions
501	Exemptions, Standard Deduction and Filing Information
502	Medical and Dental Expenses
508	Educational Expenses
521	Moving Expenses
523	Tax Information on Selling Your Home
524	Credit for the Elderly or the Disabled
525	Taxable and Nontaxable Income
527	Residential Rental Property (Including Rental of Vacation Houses)
529	Miscellaneous Deductions
545	Interest Expense
553	Highlights of the Current Year's Tax Changes
554	Tax Information for Older Americans
910	Guide to Free Tax Services
917	Business Use of a Car
920	List of Available IRS Publications
929	Tax Rules for Children and Dependents

Write to the Closest IRS Center

IRS Forms Distribution Centers

Central: P.O. Box 9903, Bloomington, IL 61799
Eastern: P.O. Box 25866, Richmond, VA 23289
Western: Rancho Cordova, CA 95743-0001

IRS Audits

The principal motivation for keeping good personal tax records is the fear of an IRS audit. The IRS conducts three basic types of audits:

1. **Correspondence audit.** This is the simplest audit and requires only that you mail in the records that support some specific claim or claims on your tax return.

2. **Field audit.** An IRS agent comes to your home or place of business to review your records.

3. **Office audit.** In this case, you must go to a local IRS office with your records. This is the most common kind of personal audit. It is usually limited to two or three specific issues, so you would not ordinarily need to bring all your records.

Certainly, the better organized your recordkeeping has been, the greater the chance that your audit will be uneventful!

Organizing Your "Stuff"

There! Now all your essential papers are safely tucked away where you can retrieve them in a moment's notice. You have set a specific time and place for paying household bills, and you've even established a manageable bill-paying routine. You are ready to move on to the wider frontiers of personal organization…putting in some sort of order all that *stuff* you keep collecting because you have so many interests and needs!

Stuff means anything from birthday cards (new or used) to travel coupons, from the kids' artwork to articles you mean to read someday. Organizing stuff doesn't have to be super sophisticated; it just needs to *work* for *you*. We don't need to go to extremes to take charge of our home life. In the movie *Accidental Tourist*, Rose organizes all the cans in her pantry alphabetically! We think the 80-20 rule is a lot more practical. If we can be 80% organized for 20% of the work, that's a good deal. Here are some ideas that work for us.

3-Ring Binders

We have found that storing things in 3-ring binders keeps our house from becoming a 3-ring circus. There's no end to the kinds of things that we can stuff between the covers of a 2" or 3" loose-leaf binder. Binders are much easier to leaf through than regular files are; we remember better what we have saved because we see it every time we flip through looking for something. Here is a list of subjects we have organized in binders.

Articles to read
Children's art/papers
Correspondence
Decorating ideas
Family history
Gardening ideas
Health & fitness
Home office ideas
Mail order catalogs
Photographs and personal mementos
Projects
Recipes
"Relatively Speaking"
Retirement ideas
Subscriptions
Upcoming events
Vacationing and travel brochures

We should explain the topic, "Relatively Speaking." Several years ago, we were feeling a little guilty about not having been in touch with our vast network of relatives during the Christmas season. When we were first married, we used to *make* gifts for *everybody*. Then, the number of in-laws, nieces and nephews began to grow geometrically. Unless we wanted to spend the whole year working as Santa's elves, we needed to change our gift-giving practice. So we began a new ritual of drawing one name each from a family lottery and exchanging a nice gift with that person. After some years and the inevitable moving of families to follow career opportunities, even the Christmas drawing somehow faded into family history. Then we came up with a great idea for a present we could give to the *whole* family.

Our present was to initiate a family newsletter called *Relatively Speaking*. We designed an 8-page format and instituted several feature columns. We called around the country for news from the 14 siblings (we both come from families of seven children), the grandmothers and the latest generation as well. Now *Relatively Speaking* has a family circulation of 82, is published three times a year (summers off) and is really fun to read. It's easily the best gift we ever made, and it all comes together in a 3-ring binder!

Supplies

To get started on organizing your stuff, gather your supplies in that time-honored home-office tool kit: the humble shoe box. Maybe you can dress it up first with some gorgeous wrapping paper, wallpaper or decorator fabric to add a touch of class to this adventure. You will want to have a pair of sharp scissors, transparent tape, reinforcing tabs, 3-inch peel-and-stick labels, a stapler and some felt tip pens. A pack of loose-leaf paper is handy for inserting notes into your collections (like reminding yourself *why* you have decided to save this or that!), and you'll need a package of those 3-hole divider pages with the plastic tabs on the edge. Get a 3-hole punch so you can prepare paper items for insertion into your binders. We have found that a single-hole punch is also handy for heavier items that can't slip into a 3-holer. Try starting with about six binders to see how you like using them.

We have a way of labeling the things that we store in binders that helps us sort and locate them later. For example, as we read through various magazines or flyers (We confess—we actually love "junk mail"), we will tear out or copy something we want to save. We staple longer articles together and punch them with three holes for the binder. Then fasten a peel-and-stick label at the top right margin and write:

Binder Subject:	Current Date:
Topic:	Discard Date:
Notes:	

For smaller items and things that would be ruined by punching holes in them, I use plastic "sheet protectors" that have three holes already punched along the edge. These are great for spare greeting cards (e.g., oh my gosh, Mike's birthday is tomorrow . . . no problem, here's a funny card!), photos, coupons, theater tickets and invitations.

Keep a few of these sheet protectors in the binder you've designated for "Upcoming Events." Then, at last, you will know where to put the invitation to the wedding that is six weeks away, the directions to next month's company picnic and the airline tickets you had to buy three months in advance to get the bargain price. Better yet, you will know where to *find* them later!

You will want to get binders that can be labeled on the spine so you can stand lots of them on the shelf and easily select the one you want. You can then store your binders on your desk top between two bookends. Even better, buy or make book shelves for your binder-files. Be sure the shelves are about 14" apart to accommodate large binders with room to spare. We think you will like this 3-hole approach to life so much that you will soon have dozens of binders, so be generous when you plan the shelf space!

Office supply and stationery stores offer binders in a rainbow of colors. You may want to organize your collections by hue. Plain binders can be less expensive, and you may want to dress them up by covering them with wrapping paper, wallpaper or some colorful fabric remnants. You can also get color-coded index kits, which you can use to create custom *indexes* inside your binders. These index kits (see our list of suppliers in the appendix) make it easy and fun to separate your articles and organize them by topic. Having an index will be helpful, too, because it causes you to put more effort into thinking about why you are saving a particular article as you fill in the index.

Tips from Mary

Card trays. A good tool for organizing ideas and some of the small items that you save is the simple file card tray for holding index cards. Trays keep things more visible and accessible than putting them in a regular file or even a 3-ring binder. Though they are called file card "trays," they look like boxes. Two unique features make them especially useful: a label frame on the front of the box and, on the inside bottom, a sliding device that allows you to adjust the size of the space.

The most popular boxes are printed with a faux-marble design, usually green. Venturesome suppliers have begun to make them available in different prints and color. Sizes range from 4" x 6" to 6" x 9" and even larger.

Greeting cards: The squirrel's way. I am a greeting card person. I really enjoy receiving cards for birthdays, holidays and special events, so I assume that my family and friends will also get a lift from timely cards saying I remembered and I cared. The only way I have been able even to approximate "keeping up" is to *stockpile* cards. When I shop, I make a point of browsing through the card racks and buying cards I like but don't necessarily need right away.

Squirrelling away cards for later use means that I don't have to make a special trip to the mall to drop a line to a sister or nephew. To make my "squirrelling away" system work, though, I needed a simple inventory system so I could retrieve an appropriate card without effort. Here's what I found works for me—

I bought a 6" x 9" file card tray and cut dividers out of old manila folders to mark four sections in the box. I use four categories:

> Birthdays
> Holidays & Holy days
> Special Events
> Thanks & Blanks

Before I settled on these, I used to try to have categories for Valentine's Day, Thanksgiving, grandmothers and about a dozen others. It got too frustrating. The four simple categories are easier to add new cards to and just as easy to retrieve them.

The "Special Events" category has cards for anniversaries, bereavement, first Communion, weddings . . . you know, life events. The "Thanks & Blanks" has "thank you" cards and a nice assortment of those beautiful cards with no preprinted verse–the "write your own message" cards.

Photos need a home too. I have dozens of albums, of course, but my album making seems to come in spurts—about once every five years! In the meantime, I accumulate thousands of likenesses that I want to keep in some kind of order…so our family can enjoy them and so when the next wave of album-making enthusiasm breaks on my shore, I'll be ready! So where do I keep them? You guessed it…in 4 x 6 file card trays.

There are probably as many ways to group family pictures as there are families. Chronological may be the easiest approach. It's fun on a snowy night to say after supper, "Hey, let's get out the pictures from the cross-country trip in '81." If your boxes are all labeled with dates, it's no trick at all to pull down a few hundred golden memories to laugh and cry over. When you get the energy to move on to albums, you might want to group your pictures by themes…Weddings, Vacations, or Homes you have lived in. But in the meantime, chronological boxes will keep the pictures in play.

THANK YOU!

We have found that getting important documents, bills and "stuff" under control has taken much of the frustration out of our daily routine and freed us to enjoy life more. Reducing all our "systems" to a book has been a stimulating adventure that we could not have experienced with *you*, our reader! It is really appropriate to thank you because we sincerely appreciate your interest in our work, and we hope that it will enhance the quality of *your* life.

For more information about how our organization's products and the Financial Advantage series of personal finance books can help you or just to share organizing tips we could use in a later edition, write to us:

Financial Advantage, Inc.
P.O. Box 1870
Ellicott City, Maryland 21041-1870

You can use this "Source Guide" to help you make your exciting journey toward financial prosperity and peace of mind. We have divided these resources into five major categories: books, magazines and newspapers, pamphlets, office products, and services and organizations. You will find resources to help you with cash management, tax planning, investing, retirement planning, estate planning, organizing important information and bill-paying, managing your time and setting goals.

Books

Altfest, Lew, and Karen Altfest, *Lew Altfest Answers Almost All Your Questions About Money,* 1992 (McGraw-Hill, Order Dept., Monterey Ave., Blue Ridge Summit, PA 17294; 800-233-1128)

Armstrong, Alexandra, and Mary R. Donahue, *On Your Own: A Widow's Passage to Emotional and Financial Well-Being,* 1993 (Dearborn Financial Publishing, 520 N. Dearborn St., Chicago, IL 60610; 800-322-8621)

Anthony, Joseph, *Kiplinger's Working for Yourself•FULL TIME•PART TIME •ANYTIME,* 1993 (Kiplinger Books, 3401 East-West Hwy., Hyattsville, MD 20782; 800-544-0155)

Berg, Adriane G., *Warning: Dying May Be Hazardous to Your Wealth,* 1992 (Hawthorn, NJ: The Career Press; 800-CAREER-1)

Berthelsen, Bert A., *How To Survive and Succeed Without A Credit Card,* 1990 (Merced, CA: Half Pint Publishing; 209-722-4456)

Bliss, Edwin, *Getting Things Done* (New York, NY: Bantam Books, 1980)

Blitz, Ed, *The 10% Solution: Your Key to Financial Security,* 1989 (McGraw-Hill, Order Dept., Monterey Ave., Blue Ridge Summit, PA 17294; 800-233-1128)

Burkett, Larry, *The Financial Planning Workbook,* 1979 (Chicago, IL: Moody Press: 800-722-1976)

Burkett, Larry, *Preparing for Retirement: Financial Security in Uncertain Times,* 1992 (Chicago, IL: Moody Press: 800-722-1976)

Burns, Robert, and Rees Johnson, *Personal Finance and Home Management: Master Forms and Contracts from Your Copier* (Tuscon, AZ: Knight-Ridder Press/HP Books, Inc., 1987)

Covey, Stephen R., *The 7 Habits of Highly Effective People: Powerful Lessons in Personal Change* (New York, NY: Fireside Book, Simon & Schuster, 1989)

Cheney, Walter J., William J. Diehm and Frank E. Seeley, *The Second 50 Years— A Reference Manual for Senior Citizens* (New York, NY: Paragon House, 1992)

Culp, Stephanie, *Conquering the Paper Pile-up,* 1990 (Cincinnati, OH: Writer's Digest Books; 800-289-0963)

Diamond, Susan Z., *Records Management,* 1991 (New York, NY: AMACOM; 800-262-9699)

Dorf, Pat, *File: Don't Pile!* (New York, NY: St. Martins Press, 1983)

Dolan, Ken and Daria, *The Smart Money Family Financial Planner* (New York, NY: Berkley Books, 1992)

Editors of Sunset Books and *Sunset* Magazine, *Home Office and Workspaces* (Menlo Park, CA: Lane Publishing Co., 1986)

Eisenberg, Ronni, with Kate Kelly, *Organize Yourself!* (New York, NY: Collier Books, Macmillan Publishing Co., 1986)

Enteen, Robert, *Health Insurance: How To Get It, Keep It, or Improve What You've Got* (New York, NY: Paragon House, 1992)

Feder, Michael E., *Money Minder: Simplify, Organize and Manage Your Personal Financial Records,* 1989 (Liberty House of McGraw-Hill, Order Dept., Monterey Ave., Blue Ridge Summit, PA 17294; 800-233-1128)

Goodman, Jordan E., and Sonny Bloch, *Everyone's Money Book,* 1994 (Dearborn Financial Publishing, 520 N. Dearborn St., Chicago, IL 60610; 800-322-8621)

Hayden, Ruth, *How To Turn Your Money Life Around: The Money Books for Women* (Deerfield Beach, FL: Health Communications, Inc., 1992)

Hemphill, Barbara, *Taming the Paper Tiger,* 1993 (Kiplinger Books, 3401 East-West Hwy., Hyattsville, MD 20782; 800-544-0155)

Heurer, Edwin R., Raymond H. Starkes III and Richard Greene, *Getting Out of Debt for Good!,* 1992 (Balanced Books, G.O.O.D., P.O. Box 1590, Annapolis, MD 21404; 800-336-3075)

Investment Company Institute, *Mutual Fund Fact Book–Industry Trends and Statistics for 1991,* 32nd Edition, 1992 (Washington, D.C.: Investment Company Institute; 202-293-7700). Also publishes excellent consumer information pamphlets on a variety of investing subjects.

Jehle, Faustin F., *The Complete and Easy Guide to Social Security and Medicare* (Madison, CT: Fraser Publishing Company, 1991)

J. K. Lasser Institute, *J.K. Lasser's Your 1992 Income Tax,* an annual edition (New York, NY: Prentice Hall Press, 1991)

Lawrence, Judy, *The Budget Kit: The Common Cent$ Money Management Workbook*, 1993 (Dearborn Financial Publishing, 520 N. Dearborn St., Chicago, IL 60610; 800-322-8621)

Little, Jeffrey B., and Lucien Rhodes, *Understanding Wall Street*, 1991 (Liberty House of McGraw-Hill, Order Dept., Monterey Ave., Blue Ridge Summit, PA 17294; 800-233-1128)

Mackenzie, R. Alec, **The Time Trap: How To Get More Done in Less Time,** 1991 (New York, NY: AMACOM; 800-262-9699)

Magee, David S. *Everything Your Heirs Need To Know: Your Assets, Family History and Final Wishes*, 1993 (Dearborn Financial Publishing, 520 N. Dearborn St., Chicago, IL 60610; 800-322-8621)

Marquis, Derek A., *Until Debt Due Us Part—Money Management Strategies for the 1990s: A Personal Finance Course* (Salt Lake, UT: D.C. International, 1989)

Martin, J. Michael, *Life after CDs: A Practical Guide to Safe Investing,* 1993 (Dearborn Financial Publishing, 520 N. Dearborn St., Chicago, IL 60610; 800-322-8621)

Martindale, Judith A., and Mary J. Moses, *Creating Your Own Future,* 1991 (Naperville, IL: Sourcebooks Trade; 708-961-2161)

Mayer, Jeffrey J., *If You Haven't Got the Time To Do It Right, When Will You Find the Time To Do It Over?* (New York, NY: Simon & Schuster, 1990)

McAleese, Tama, *Money: How To Get It, Keep It and Make It Grow,* 1991 (Hawthorne, NJ: The Career Press; 800-CAREER-1)

McCormally, Kevin, *Kiplinger's Sure Ways To Cut Your Taxes–1992,* 1991 (Kiplinger Books, 3401 East-West Hwy., Hyattsville, MD 20782; 800-544-0155)

Miller, Ruth Wagner, *The Time Minder–Making Time Work for You* (Chappaqua, NY: Christian Herald Books, 1980)

Miller, Theodore J., *Kiplinger's Make Your Money Grow,* 1988 (Kiplinger Books, 3401 East-West Hwy., Hyattsville, MD 20782; 800-544-0155)

Miller, Theodore J., *Kiplinger's Invest Your Way to Wealth,* 1991 (Kiplinger Books, 3401 East-West Hwy., Hyattsville, MD 20782; 800-544-0155)

Moe, Harold, *Making Your Paycheck Last*, 1993 (Holmen, WI: Harsand Financial Press; 800-526-3848)

Morris, Kenneth M., and Alan M. Siegel, *The Wall Street Journal–Guide To Understanding Personal Finance* (New York, NY: Lightbulb Press, Simon & Schuster, 1992)

Moskowitz, Robert, *How To Organize Your Work and Your Life: Proven Time Management Techniques for Business, Professional and Other Busy People* (Garden City, NY: Dolphin Book, Doubleday & Company, 1981)

Pollar, Odette, *Organizing Your Workspace: A Guide to Personal Productivity,* 1992, Fifty-Minute Series Book (Menlo Park, CA: CRISP Publications, 800-442-7477)

Quinn, Jane Bryant, *Making the Most of Your Money: Smart Ways To Create Wealth and Plan Your Finances in the '90s* (New York, NY: Simon & Schuster, 1991)

Shear, Carolyn and Elliott Shear, *The Health Insurance Claims Kit,* 1992 (Dearborn Financial Publishing, 520 N. Dearborn St., Chicago, IL 60610; 800-322-8621)

Silver, Susan, *Organized To Be the Best!–New Timesaving Ways To Simplify and Improve How You Work,* 1991 (Los Angeles, CA: Adams-Hall Publishing; 800-888-4452)

Skousen, Mark, and Jo Ann Skousen, *High Finance on a Low Budget,* 1993 (Dearborn Financial Publishing, 520 N. Dearborn St., Chicago, IL 60610; 800-322-8621)

Sloane, Leonard, *The New York Times Book of Personal Finance* (New York, NY: Times Books, Random House, 1992)

The Smart Consumer's Directory–1993 Edition (Nashville, TN: Thomas Nelson Publishers, 1992)

Staff of *Changing Times* Magazine, *Kiplinger's Buying & Selling a Home,* 1990 (Kiplinger Books, 3401 East-West Hwy., Hyattsville, MD 20782; 800-544-0155)

Unger, Robert M. & John H. Kupillas, Jr., *Tune In to Success* (New York, NY: Wynwood Press, 1991)

Updegrave, Walter L., *How To Keep Your Savings Safe: Protecting the Money You Can't Afford To Lose* (New York, NY: Crown Publishers, 1992)

Ventura, John, *Fresh Start! Surviving Money Troubles, Rebuilding Your Credit, Recovering before or after Bankruptcy,* 1992 (Dearborn Financial Publishing, 520 N. Dearborn St., Chicago, IL 60610; 800-322-8621)

Ventura, John, *The Credit Repair Kit,* 1993 (Dearborn Financial Publishing, 520 N. Dearborn St., Chicago, IL 60610; 800-322-8621)

Williamson, Gordon K., *Low Risk Investing: How To Get a Good Return on Your Money Without Losing Any Sleep,* 1993 (Holbrook, MA: Bob Adams Publishers; 800-872-5627)

Winston, Stephanie, *The Organized Executive: New Ways To Manage Time, Paper and People* (New York, NY: Warner Books, 1983)

Wurman, Richard Saul, Alan Siegel, Kenneth M. Morris, *The Wall Street Journal–Guide To Understanding Money & Markets* (New York, NY: Access Press, 1990)

Magazines and Newspapers

Many magazines cover personal finance. Check your library for others. These will get you started.

AAII Journal (*American Association of Individual Investors,* 625 N. Michigan Ave., Chicago, IL 60611; 312-280-0170). Monthly investment and money management articles.

Kiplinger's Personal Finance **Magazine** (3401 East-West Highway, Editors Park, MD 20782; 800-544-0155). Monthly investment and money management articles.

Money **Magazine** (Money, P. O. Box 60001, Tampa, FL 33660-0001; 800-633-9970) Monthly investment and money management articles.

The Wall Street Journal (200 Burnett Rd., Chicopee, MA 01020; 800-JOURNAL). Daily newspaper for personal and business financial news.

Worth **Magazine** (82 Devonshire St., Route 25A, Boston, MA 12109; 800-777-1851). Monthly investment and money management articles.

Pamphlets

Many publications are available from the U.S. government printing press. **The** *Consumer Information Catalog* lists approximately 200 free or low-cost federal booklets with helpful information for consumers. This free catalog is published quarterly by the Consumer Information Center of the U.S. General Services Administration. You can order single copies of the catalog (Catalog, Consumer Information Center, Pueblo, CO 81009; 719-948-4000).

For **IRS publications**, see Chapter 9, "The IRS and Your Files!" for the address to send for publications from your area of the country.

If you are in need of specific IRS tax forms, call 800-TAX FORM.

Office Products

Stores

Most filing supplies that you need are available in your local office supply stores. The small local stores have always carried a large variety of office supplies. The large office superstores and discount stores often have increasingly good buys especially on mass-produced items. Also, many office supply catalogs require bulk orders of items to be cost effective.

Chapter 2, "Getting Started," helps you choose filing cabinets and supplies. Below are listed some manufacturers who offer office supplies, accessories and equipment. They sell directly to consumers via mail order, or they give product information and names of local dealers on their toll-free line. Some of these major manufacturers of filing equipment and supplies offer products that are readily available in most office superstores and mass market stores.

Manufacturers

These manufacturers sell office products that are designed for home use. Most of their products are readily available in stores in your area. Call for information and a local dealer.

Anthes Universal (Pelican, Inc., Shelbyville, IN 46176; 800-387-2364). Sells large variety of file and office accessories, boxes, storage files.

Avery (Div. Consumer Service Center, P.O. Box 5244, Diamond Bar, CA 91765-4000; 800-642-8379). Offers file labels and index kits for binders.

Fellowes (1789 Norwood Ave., Itasca, IL 60143-1095; 800-955-3344). Sells bill payment box, assorted file and file storage boxes and accessories.

Hon Industries (800-654-5132). Sells mainly commercial file cabinets, some for home use as well.

Esselte Pendaflex (Clinton Rd., Garden City, NY 11530; 516-741-3200). Offers hanging files and folders, handy organizers, file boxes and related accessories.

GMI-America's Home Organizer (P. O. Box 557 McKee Rd., Dover, DE 19903; 800-441-7428). Sells steel file cabinets and stackable cube storage units.

Rubbermaid Office Supplies (800-827-5060). Has file boxes, files and accessories. Call for information on a dealer near you.

Sentry (Sentry Group, 900 Linden Ave., Rochester, NY 14625; 800-828-1438). Offers fireproof safes and boxes for home and office use.

Trav-L-File (8855 Cypress Woods Dr., Olive Branch, MS 38654; 800-826-8806). Sells portable file boxes, rolling file shuttle for legal or letter size.

Catalogs/Direct Mail

Anticipations (9 Ross Simmons Dr., Cranston, RI 02920-4476; 800-556-7376). Features Queen Ann-styled file cabinets.

Hold Everything (P.O. Box 7807, San Francisco, CA 94120; 800-421-2264). Offers a varity of organizing containers for home use.

Lillian Vernon (Virginia Beach, VA 23479; 804-430-5555). Carries office accessories for home use.

Orvis (800-541-3541). Sells oak Shaker furniture file cabinets.

The Paragon (89 Tom Harvey Rd., Westerly, RI 02891; 800-343-3095). Offers Queen Ann-styled file cabinets and other supplies.

The Personal Touch (Artistic Greetings, Inc., P. O. Box 1623, Elmira, NY 14902; 607-733-6313). Sells personalized stationery and desk accessories.

Quill (P.O. Box 4700, Lincolnshire, IL 60197-5708; 708- 634-4800). Carries office supplies and equipment.

Reliable Home Office (P.O. Box 1501, Ottawa, IL 61350-9916; 800- 869-6000). Stocks office supplies and equipment.

Signatures (19465 Brennan Ave., Perris, CA 92379; 800-943-2021). Offers attractive filing cabinets—special styles.

Visible (1750 Wallace Ave., St. Charles, IL 60174; 800-323-0628). Sells office supplies and equipment.

Yield House (Dept. 6850, P.O. Box 5000, North Conway, NH 03860; 800-258-4720). Sells home-styled oak and pine file cabinets in either unfinished kits or fully finished.

Photographic Organization Supplies and Equipment (Mail Order)

Creative Memories (41 W. 8th Ave., Oshkosh, WI 54906; 203-854-1610). Local representatives give seminars and workshops on creating unique photo albums.

Exposures (1 Memory La., Oshkosh, WI 54903; 800-222-4947)

Light Impressions (P. O. Box 940, 439 Monroe Ave., Rochester, NY 14603; 800-828-6216)

20th Century Plastics (3628 Crenshaw Blvd., Los Angeles, CA 90016; 800-767-0777)

Pioneer Photo Albums, Inc. (P.O. Box 2497, Chatsworth, CA 91311; 800-423-5999)

Specialty Stationery and Papers

American Stationery Co. Inc. (100 Park Ave., Peru, Indiana 46970; 800-822-2577). Sells stationery, accessories and supplies.

Deluxe Business Forms and Supplies (1125 Kelly Johnson Blvd., Colorado Springs, CO 80920; 800-843-4294). Carries forms, checks and rubber stamps.

The Writewell Co. (919 Transit Building, 5850 W. 80th St, Indianapolis, IN 46268; 317-871-6700). Offers stationery, accessories and supplies.

Paper Direct, Inc. (205 Chubb Ave., Lyndhurst, NJ 07071; 800-A-PAPERS). Carries a variety of paper supplies and accessories.

Services and Organizations

American Bar Association (ABA, 1800 M Street, N. W. , Washington, DC 20036; 202-331-2297)

American Institute of Certified Public Accountants (AICPA, 1211 Avenue of the Americas, New York, NY 10036-8775). Provides information on looking for an accountant and offers a series of "Consumer Guides" on a variety of subjects, such as "Personal Finances" and "Managing Credit."

Association of Records Managers and Administrators, Inc. (ARMA International, 4200 Somerset, Suite 215, Prairie Village, KS 66208; 800-422-2762). This is the major association that sets the guidelines for all business filing.

Consumer Credit Counseling Service (CCCS). Nonprofit organization that provides money management techniques, debt payment plans and educational programs. You can find the CCCS office nearest you by contacting the National Foundation for Consumer Credit, Inc. (8611 2nd Ave., Suite 100, Silver Spring, MD 20910-3372; 800-388-CCCS). Many other organizations, including credit unions, family service centers and religious organizations that offer some type of free or low-cost credit counseling as well.

Institute of Certified Financial Planners (ICFP, 7600 E. Eastman Ave., Suite 301, Denver, CO 80231; 303-751-7600 or fax: 800-322-4237)

National Association of Personal Financial Advisors (NAPFA, 1130 Lake Cook Rd., Suite 150, Buffalo Grove, IL 60089; 800-366-2732). Call for referral to a local fee-only financial adviser, and a questionnaire to help decide on an adviser.

National Association of Professional Organizers (NAPO, 655 N. Alvernon, Suite 108, Tucson, AZ 85711; 602-322-9753) Professional organizers, also gives seminars on organization of papers. Call for names of professional organizers in your area or Information.

Padgett-Thompson Div/AMA (American Management Association, P. O. Box 8297, Shawnee Mission, KS 66208; 800-255-4141). Offers seminars on record organization and time management.

SkillPath, Inc. (6900 Squibb Rd., Mission, KS 66201; 800-873-7545). Gives seminars on organizing and record organization.

Index

Order Form

Financial Advantage, Inc.
P.O. Box 1870
Ellicott City, Maryland 21041-1870
Toll-Free *Order* number 800-695-3453
Customer Service number 800-466-3453

Please Ship To:
Name _____
Company _____
Address _____
City/State/Zip _____

Item	Quantity	Description	Unit Price	Amount
503		Life after CDs: A Practical Guide to Safe Investing (book)	19.95	
501		Home Filing Made Easy! (book)	15.95	
203		FINANCIAL PLANNING ORGANIZER (kit)	19.95	
301		BILL PAYER™ (kit)	19.95	

Sub Total

Sales Tax (MD residents plaese add 5%)

Shipping* (UPS sorry no P.O. Boxes)

TOTAL

__ Check enclosed

__ Please charge my:
   __ VISA
   __ MasterCard

Account # _____ Exp. Date _____

Signature _____

Shipping 2.50 for one book, 3.50 for one kit. If you order two or more items, we pay the shipping!

Thank You for Your Order.

Order Form

Financial Advantage, Inc.
P.O. Box 1870
Ellicott City, Maryland 21041-1870
Toll-Free *Order* number 800-695-3453
Customer Service number 800-466-3453

Please Ship To:
Name _____
Company _____
Address _____
City/State/Zip _____

Item	Quantity	Description	Unit Price	Amount
503		Life after CDs: A Practical Guide to Safe Investing (book)	19.95	
501		Home Filing Made Easy! (book)	15.95	
203		FINANCIAL PLANNING ORGANIZER (kit)	19.95	
301		BILL PAYER™ (kit)	19.95	

Sub Total

Sales Tax (MD residents plaese add 5%)

Shipping* (UPS sorry no P.O. Boxes)

TOTAL

__ Check enclosed

__ Please charge my:
   __ VISA
   __ MasterCard

Account # _____ Exp. Date _____

Signature _____

Shipping 2.50 for one book, 3.50 for one kit. If you order two or more items, we pay the shipping!

Thank You for Your Order.

From the Financial Advantage Series . . .
Two new books to simplify your financial life and enhance your prosperity

Life after CDs: A Practical Guide To Safe Investing

- Perhaps your greatest financial challenge is saving and investing for a secure future.

- Puzzled about how to respond to today's low interest rates?

Here is a personal finance classic . . .
Using simple graphs and everyday language, this book walks you through the basics of mutual funds and government bonds. It teaches you how to find a wise advisor you can trust, shows you the only mutual fund company you'll ever need, tells you how to plan for retirement and how to earn 7%, 10%, and 12% a year . . . *safely!*

308 pages of savvy for the conservative investor
Item # 503 ....*$19.95*

Home Filing Made Easy!

If you like our comprehensive guidance on filing and paying bills, think how much your family and friends would appreciate receiving it from you. A unique gift for parents, friends, and your grown children; helps starts them off on the right track.

Item #501 ....*$15.95*

Two practical products from the HOMEFILE® division of Financial Advantage, Inc. that will make it easy to take charge of all your important papers, taxes, and bills.

FINANCIAL PLANNING ORGANIZER KIT

For the ultimate in simple, beautiful, orderly files! Includes:

22 sturdy, colorful file divider cards, each card is pre-printed with category names and complete information on what to keep and how long to keep it. Also comes with handbook containing valuable data collection center.

Item # 223 ....$19.95

BILL PAYER™

Your monthly bill-paying routine will come together in this handsome faux-marble bill caddy.
- Compartments for pens, stamps, envelopes and calculators.
- Folders for unpaid bills, credit card reciepts and checking account statements.
- Monthly folder forms for tracking bills and storing receipts.

Item #301 ....$19.95